AMERICAN AUTHORS
AND CRITICS SERIES

GENERAL EDITOR

JOHN MAHONEY

University of Detroit

ERNEST HEMINGWAY IN 1957

ERNEST
HEMINGWAY

An Introduction and Interpretation

SHERIDAN BAKER

The University of Michigan

HOLT, RINEHART AND WINSTON, INC.

New York · Chicago · San Francisco · Toronto · London

*Barnes & Noble, Inc., is the exclusive distribu-
tor of the hard-bound edition of this title.*

Acknowledgment is made to Jonathan Cape, Ltd., to Charles Scribner's Sons, and to the Executors of the Ernest Hemingway Estate for
permission to quote from the following works by Ernest Hemingway:
Across the River and into the Trees (Copyright 1950, Ernest Hemingway); *Death in the Afternoon* (Copyright 1932, Charles Scribner's
Sons; copyright © renewed 1960, Ernest Hemingway); *A Farewell
to Arms* (Copyright 1929, Charles Scribner's Sons; copyright © renewed 1957, Ernest Hemingway); *The Fifth Column and the First
Forty-nine Stories* (Copyright 1938, Ernest Hemingway; copyright
© renewed 1966, Mary Hemingway); *For Whom the Bell Tolls*
(Copyright 1940, Ernest Hemingway); *Green Hills of Africa* (Copy-
right 1935, Charles Scribner's Sons; copyright © renewed 1963,
Mary Hemingway); *The Sun Also Rises* (Copyright 1926, Charles
Scribner's Sons; copyright renewed 1954, Ernest Hemingway); *To
Have and Have Not* (Copyright 1937, Ernest Hemingway; copy-
right © renewed 1965, Mary Hemingway); *The Old Man and the
Sea* (Copyright 1952, Ernest Hemingway); *The Short Stories of
Ernest Hemingway* (Copyright 1925, 1926, 1927, 1932, 1933, Charles
Scribner's Sons; copyright renewed 1953, 1954, © 1955, 1960, 1961,
Ernest Hemingway; 1961, Mary Hemingway. Copyright 1936,
Ernest Hemingway; copyright © renewed 1964, Mary Hemingway).

Acknowledgment is also made to Miss Janet F. White, Reference
Librarian, The University of Michigan.

To my father

ABOUT THE AUTHOR

SHERIDAN BAKER, a former Fulbright lecturer at the University of Nagoya, Japan, is Professor of English at the University of Michigan. He has been President of the Michigan Academy of Science, Arts, and Letters and editor of the *Papers* of that Academy. He is editor of the *Michigan Quarterly Review*. Professor Baker has published *The Practical Stylist, The Essayist, The Complete Stylist* and scholarly papers on Fielding, Richardson, Johnson, Smollett, Cummings, Catullus, Hemingway, and Alan Paton. His poetry has appeared in *The New Yorker* and other magazines.

CONTENTS

ILLUSTRATIONS

CHRONOLOGY

1899   Ernest Miller Hemingway born July 21, in Oak Park, Illinois, second of six children and eldest son of Clarence Edmunds Hemingway and Grace Hall Hemingway.

1916   "Judgment of Manitou," his first story, published in *Tabula*, literary magazine of Oak Park High School, in February.

1917   Graduated from Oak Park High School in June; rejected by army for poor vision in one eye. Cub reporter for Kansas City *Star* in the fall.

1918   While on Red Cross canteen duty, badly wounded (July 8) by explosion of a mortar shell at Fossalta di Piave, Italy. Removed to a hospital in Milan.

1919   January 21, landed in New York and returned home to Oak Park to convalesce. Joined staff of Toronto *Star Weekly*.

1920   February 14, wrote his first article for the Toronto *Star*.

1921   September 3, married to Hadley Richardson at Horton's Bay, Michigan. December 8, sailed with bride for Paris as correspondent for the Toronto *Star*.

1923   First trip to Spain and the bullfights in the spring. *Three Stories and Ten Poems*, his first book, published midsummer in Paris, containing "Up in Michigan," "Out of Season," "My Old Man." First son, John Hadley Nicanor, born in Toronto, October 10.

1924   *in our time*, 170 copies, published in Paris (spring).

1925   "The Undefeated" (entitled "Stierkampf") published in *Der Querschnitt* in the summer; *In Our Time* published in New York, October 5.

1926   *The Torrents of Spring* published on May 28; *The Sun Also Rises*, on October 22.

1927   Divorced Hadley Richardson, March 10. Married Pauline Pfeiffer. *Men Without Women* published on October 14. Began residence in Key West, Florida.

1928   Patrick, second son, born in Kansas City, June 30; Dr.

C. E. Hemingway, father, committed suicide, December 6.

1929   *A Farewell to Arms* published on September 27.

1930   Automobile accident and hospitalization in Billings, Montana, in November.

1932   *Death in the Afternoon* published on September 23.

1933   *Winner Take Nothing* published on October 27. Began writing for *Esquire*. Safari in Africa in mid-December.

1934   Amoebic dysentery and flight past Kilimanjaro in January; completed hunting in February; returned to Key West in April.

1935   *Green Hills of Africa* published on October 25.

1936   "The Snows of Kilimanjaro," published in *Esquire,* August, and "The Short Happy Life of Francis Macomber," in *Cosmopolitan* in September.

1937   Sailed for Spain, February 27, as a correspondent for North American Newspaper Alliance, intending to raise money for ambulances for the Loyalists, and to make a documentary film, *The Spanish Earth*. *To Have and Have Not* published on October 15.

1938   *The Fifth Column and the First Forty-nine Stories* published on October 14.

1940   *For Whom the Bell Tolls* published on October 21. Divorced Pauline Pfeiffer on November 4; married Martha Gellhorn on November 21.

1941   Covered Sino-Japanese War from Hong Kong.

1942   Settled at Finca Vigia, his villa in Cuba. Departed to cover World War II for *Collier's*.

1945   Divorced Martha Gellhorn on December 21.

1946   Married Mary Welsh on March 14 in Havana.

1950   *Across the River and into the Trees* published on September 7.

1952   *The Old Man and the Sea* published on September 1 in *Life,* and on September 8 by Scribner's.

1953   Received the Pulitzer Prize for *The Old Man and the Sea*.

1954   Awarded the Nobel Prize for "forceful and style-making mastery of the art of modern narration."

1961   Committed suicide at home near Ketchum, Idaho, July 2.

1964   *A Moveable Feast* published on May 5.

INTRODUCTION

HEMINGWAY is a limited writer. But he has knocked his way among the immortals by his tight, poignant style, giving the young twentieth century a voice and a manner. He is a journalist transforming the report into art. He is a boy eternally trying to prove himself a man. He is modern man, driven by a warring world to survive in himself. He is the existential battler, the knight in the turtle-necked sweater, who has discovered the ultimate romance in fighting hopeless odds among the ashes of our temples.

And because we all respond to the romantic dream of embattled self, which is at the center of Hemingway's best work, Hemingway will continue to be read and will continue, in his way, to be great. He has found, in himself, our own soft romantic center, our sweet dream of despair, and toughened it into bravery. He has caught man's essential nagging belief—aggravated by a nihilistic, skeptical, and uncertain period—that we do not get all we deserve, that we are made for something better than brutality and death, that our virtues ought to be rewarded by some supreme and deathless love and by some grandeur that neither the rubble of two wars nor the glitter of the suburbs can supply.

Hemingway is the apostle of the faith that is lost, the faith that had already begun to erode by the middle of the nineteenth century. He is the American expression of the British Henley who wrote:

> Out of the night that covers me,
> Black as the Pit from pole to pole,
> I thank whatever gods may be
> For my unconquerable soul.

Like Henley, the Hemingway hero tends to be covered by night; he, too, neither winces nor cries aloud. But only late in his career does Hemingway's hero acquire anything like an unconquerable soul, as the unbowed head is bloodied. The soul of his early hero is conquered indeed, and he moves as if stunned.

Early and late, Hemingway's God is only a forlorn possibility. The sea of Christian faith had drained away over the edges of the modern world, as Matthew Arnold had perceived in "Dover Beach"

I

a half-century earlier (Philip Young also sees Arnold's pertinence), leaving neither joy, nor love, nor light, nor certitude, nor peace, nor help for pain—leaving nothing but a cry for constancy between a man and a woman standing on a darkening plain

> Swept with confused alarms of struggle and flight,
> Where ignorant armies clash by night.

Hemingway has toughened up all this to our taste. And he will continue to speak for the lost pitiful soul in all of us, as we cry out against a world that occasionally seems incapable of giving us what we so deeply and selfishly want—an attitude disguised in a brave way, in a far land, so that we can have our romance without noticing it and can believe that we are being real and tough.

Self-pity remains at the Hemingway core, but the surface is progressively covered over by a rind of courage. A tougher hero begins to predominate. Hemingway's early hero, to simplify, personifies self-pity; his later one personifies courage. The early one is beaten and passive; the later one stays unbeaten because active. The early one is young; the later one is (at least as youth would see him) old. Philip Young has taken the first hero as the only one, has seen the second only as a subsidiary figure, a "code hero," and has seen Hemingway's growth in the true hero's ability to learn the code. And certainly Mr. Young has been illuminating. I have indeed despaired of acknowledging his work—and that of Carlos Baker and Charles Fenton—in any just detail. Nevertheless, I prefer to see in Hemingway two different modes, the soft and the hard, the inner and the outer, and to see two distinct heroes—the early, beaten one, and the emerging unbeaten one, the man who is, in Hemingway's own term, "undefeated" in spite of loss.

Hemingway's early hero, Nick Adams and his successors, is a young man blown out of society and belief by shellfire in the First World War. The world now seems cruel, whimsical, senseless, with no meaning nor plan. However bleak, the energy and truth in these early stories comes from the state of mind of the young hero. We can accept the hero's attitude of defeat, his sad, drifting despair—because he is young. These stories of the defeated hero tell in extreme form the sadness and disillusion that any young person knows at some time or another, in some way or another, as he wakes up into life. The First World War simply put this disillusion on Hemingway and his generation in a sudden and shocking way. And Hemingway's fictive transposition is memorable and probably enduring. This is Hemingway's first mode. The tune is soft, sad, and sweet.

But Hemingway's second mode is different. The irony has a braver twang. Although "The Undefeated" appears early (summer, 1925)—indeed even several months before Nick Adams and *In Our Time* reached print—the undefeated mode develops slowly, not predominating until *To Have and Have Not* (1935). But thereafter the undefeated loser is Hemingway's hero, though rendered imperfect by streaks of the old defeat, until his triumph in *The Old Man and the Sea*. The undefeated loser represents an existential step up from the depths, or forward from the wall. If man seems to be beaten by a world without meaning, at least he has his courage, at least he can act. As John Killinger has recently shown in *Hemingway and the Dead Gods*, Hemingway has a great deal of the existentialist in him. Hemingway's existentialistic affirmation, however, is late, and it is further qualified by the fact that his undefeated losers, at their strongest, are all men of the lower classes, men of limited understanding, unable to see the world widely enough, it seems, to despair of hopeless situations. When Hemingway tries to move his undefeated man up the scale of intelligence, he loses him in the old Hemingway; we hear the old inner murmur of self-pity.

To see Hemingway as a writer of two opposing modes, never happily reconciled, may prove helpful. In fact, this duality of modes matches exactly the slightly schizophrenic personality apparent in Hemingway from the first, as Robert McAlmon's remembrance of the young Hemingway in Paris suggests:

> Hemingway was a type not easy to size up. At times he was deliberately hard-boiled and case-hardened; again he appeared deliberately innocent, sentimental, the hurt, soft, but fairly sensitive boy trying to conceal hurt, wanting to be brave, not bitter or cynical but being somewhat of both, and somehow on the defensive, suspicions lurking in his peering analytic glances at a person with whom he was talking. He approached a café with a small-boy, tough-guy swagger, and before strangers of whom he was doubtful a potential snarl of scorn played on his large-lipped, rather loose mouth.

The very tension in Hemingway's prose expresses his struggle to keep himself together, to integrate the soft and the hard, to heal the abysmal uncertainty. And so the undefeated loser emerges in Hemingway's works as a sign of confidence and maturity, never wholly won. The undefeated loser may serve as an index for some of Hemingway's failures and may help to distinguish some of his triumphs, played on one string or the other.

YOUNG MAN WITH A TYPEWRITER

OAK PARK

STYLE IS THE MAN, as Philip Young has observed of Hemingway. And the eighteenth-century epigram fits the twentieth-century champ like a glove. From the first, Hemingway's personal mission has been to find the style, to become the man. In his high-school activities and his high-school writing, the uneasy quest is already apparent. In his English class he is already talking about "an author's style," to the mystification of his classmates. He is already trying styles for himself. By his junior year he has a typewriter on the third floor of his family's big home in Oak Park, Illinois—conveniently remote from his prosperous, prominent family. He is already cultivating the manly arts, hunting and fishing in upper Michigan in the summer, going out for sports in the winter, taking boxing lessons in a Chicago gym. He is running away from home.

The boy was rebelling, naturally. But his rebellion was to grow into a discipline, a way of living and writing. He was to bring the athletic outdoor competitor under the close schooling of his prose. He was to become a writer, which, in the twentieth century, is to make a profession of alienation. To prove his manhood he must step outside a society that seemed to demand no proof. To cast a true line he must step clear of the formal elegancies.

The high-school boy seems conventional enough. His few decampments were brief and apparently insignificant. He was graduated at eighteen, popular and with a good record. He was cheery, amiable, remembered as always laughing. He had been a member of the debating club, the oratorical club, and the Boy's High School Club which presented talks on Christianity and the good boy's life. He had been track manager, swimmer, captain of the water basketball team, member of the championship football squad. He had been an outstanding and original student in English courses that encouraged fiction. He had been a contributor to the literary magazine, a sports reporter, editor, and wit on the school paper, and a member of the Story Club, into which the senior English teacher invited her promising students.

All this with a proper air of adolescent indifference. Hemingway's teachers themselves submitted for him his three stories and four poems to appear in *Tabula,* the school's literary magazine, relieving the author from having to seem to care. But in his private third-floor workshop, he read his things to a friend with enthusiasm. Although he later declared that football was a chore, forced on him by his size and the Oak Park system, and "did not interest me really," his lines of "Athletic Verse" (written with a teammate) make a grim glory of the mud and sweat, which is still apparent in the satirical attack on football in *The Torrents of Spring* and in a vivid reminiscence in *The Sun Also Rises*. His high-school writing is all aggressively masculine and "unliterary." Something of the bravado of indifference, the bravado of scorn for anything literary or soft, persists in Hemingway's public declarations and tight prose.

But he acknowledges his literary debts and the value of his English courses at Oak Park High School. This was to be the end of his formal schooling, but the composition classes immediately opened an opportunity to express his outdoor ruggedness, and the curriculum in English literature was unusually broad and thorough. One of his classmates found an advanced course at the University of Chicago a mere repetition of Oak Park High. Literary echoes and allusions in Hemingway's work are surprisingly persistent for one who seems, on the surface, so pugnaciously unliterary.

The Oak Park teachers encouraged Hemingway's inconoclastic flair, encouraged his parodies of the literature they taught, and almost turned him into a poet in the process. While the rest of the class struggled to create in the approved ways, Hemingway subverted assignments with stories of violence or burlesque poems—which his teachers praised and gave to the literary magazine. Hemingway's long flirtation with poetry began with one of Miss Margaret Dixon's annual assignments. Hemingway's forty-eight line parody of Kipling, "How Ballad Writing Affects Our Seniors," begins, and continues, like this:

> Oh, I've never writ a ballad
> And I'd rather eat shrimp salad
> (Tho' the Lord knows how I hate the
> Pink and Scrunchy little beasts),
> But Miss Dixon says I gotto—
> (And I pretty near forgotto)
> But I'm sitting at my table
> And my feet are pointing east.

The writer at work: with his feet pointing in the direction they eventually were to go, as they left the conventions of Oak Park and formal literature behind—Hemingway, the ironically harried hero of his own piece.

Parody is a convenient way of writing literature as one repudiates it, a contest with a master, a defeat of a champion. It indicates a grudging admiration. It also indicates an awareness of style, of words and rhythms. Poetry demands the same. From his ballad, Hemingway went on to further engagements: a parody of James Whitcomb Riley; the three-piece football poem ("The Tackle," "The Punt," "The Safety Man"), in the free modern manner of Carl Sandburg; a mildly proletarian rhymed vignette of a stoker—with the poet now entirely on his own. Both the parodic and the serious were to continue in Hemingway's poetry for the next dozen years. But his high-school poems, from laboring balladeer to laboring stoker, are already striking Hemingway's essential subject: man unappreciated. Playful or serious, at writing desk, gridiron, or furnace, where "it's hotter than hell to a man alive," the protagonist sweats for an oblivious audience, an audience worthless because it cannot know the agony.

Oak Park was also making direct impressions on Hemingway's prose. The deepest and subtlest is that of the Bible. One of his freshman texts was *Old Testament Narratives*. Later he declared, "that's how I learned to write—by reading the Bible," adding that he meant the Old Testament. Not that he started by conscious imitation. He was certainly unaware at first. But, along with his ironic and nostalgic Christian allusions, a Biblical pulsation soon becomes apparent in his mature prose; the Bible's simple repetitive understatements, paced by the incantatory *And,* soon began to reinforce the tendencies Hemingway shows from the first.

Hemingway's determination to be tough and different from his classmates immediately led him away from elegance and toward the emphasis of a limited, repetitive vocabulary. Unlike most beginners, Hemingway did not have to struggle out of hand-me-downs too big for him. He started stripped. Later he learned to enrich his prose and lengthen his sentences without losing his grip. But in his three high-school stories the prose is already pared. The subjects are savage. The dialogue is terse and colloquial—maximum effect with minimum explanation, understatement with suggestive power. The stories look like typical high-school pieces, very short, scarcely more than a single six-by-nine page, with title elaborately lettered, by a fellow student, against an illustrative vista.

The stories are self-conscious, and bold with horrifics. But they also clearly contain the later Hemingway. "Judgment of Manitou, by Ernest Hemingway, '17" (February, 1916) begins: "Dick Haywood buttoned the collar of his mackinaw up about his ears, took down his rifle from the deer horns above the fireplace of the cabin and pulled on his heavy fur mittens."

The story is nicely ironic. Pierre thinks Dick has stolen his wallet. He has set a snare for him along the trapping line. Just as Dick is jerked into the air heel first among the encircling white wolves, Pierre, back in the cabin, sees a squirrel gnawing on the remains of his wallet. He rushes frantically to the rescue but finds ravens rising from "the shapeless something that had once been Dick Haywood," catches himself in the bear trap Dick was about to tend, and accepts the judgment of Manitou at his own hands. The story ends:

> "It is the judgment of Manitou; I will save My-in-gan, the wolf, the trouble."
>
> And he reached for the rifle.

Here, in his first story, is the irony of man trapped by unjust circumstances that will pervade Hemingway's universe until he dies. Here, more startling, is the suicide to avoid tortured death that is later to haunt Hemingway's imagination, long before his father's suicide gave it illustration, and long before his own—both of them being, as Robert Jordan will say in *For Whom the Bell Tolls,* suicides "to avoid torture." Here the spare objective Hemingway is clearly in outline, in spite of bald references to the "silent places" of Jack London, in spite of "Holy quill pigs, but it's cold," and in spite of a vague North with awkward pidgin French and synthetic Indian lore.

"A Matter of Colour" (April, 1916) is a poorer thing, though an advance, in its attempt to reproduce the idiom of the Chicago gym and to get at character through speech: " 'Well, son, that kid I was just giving the lesson to reminded me of the Big Swede that gummed the best frame-up we ever almost pulled off.' " But the whole story depends on a poor joke in the last line. Bob Armstrong has signed his white protégé to fight a formidable Negro. The contract includes a forfeit for nonfulfillment. The white man hurts his wrist on a punching bag. But the fight will be on an old stage, so Bob

7

hires the Swede to club the Negro from behind the curtains when the white man gets him on the ropes. The Swede hits the wrong man, and the story ends "I bane color Blind!"

The lame joke aside, the story is a big step away from the Great White North and toward the authentic. Hemingway has soaked up the lore, and some of the speech, of the boxing world, foreshadowing "Fifty Grand" (1927) and, to some extent, "The Battler" (1925). This is the first tentative note of the "undefeated" mode. With Bob Armstrong's "Well, son," Hemingway has put himself—the high-school boy taking boxing lessons—fleetingly into fictional disguise for the first time.

The same can be seen in "Sepi Jingan" (November, 1916), the last and best of Hemingway's high-school stories. Again we have a dialect speaker telling the story to a half-autobiographical "I." The scene is Hemingway's summer country at Horton's Bay, identified only by natural, offhand hints. The narrator is an Indian who is to appear briefly, and slightly changed, in "The Doctor and the Doctor's Wife" (1924): "Billy Tabeshaw, long, lean, copper-colored, hamfaced and Ojibway." Hemingway is now, as he was not, altogether, in "A Matter of Colour," letting his fiction arise directly from close and familiar observation: "Bill is not the redskin of the popular magazine. He never says 'ugh.' I have yet to hear him grunt or speak of the Great Father at Washington." He has a humorous fancy for Peerless tobacco, his every remark leading to its commendation. Billy and "I" sit on a bank in the moonlight watching Sepi Jingan, Billy's wolfish white dog (domesticated from Hemingway's first story). Billy and his dog have tracked Paul Black Bird, a murderer, all through Canada and back into this Michigan village. On the Fourth of July, Paul drinks, which only makes him murderous and playful. He comes out of hiding, knocks Billy down as he walks along the railroad tracks, and taunts him with the original murder weapon: " 'He kept prodding me with the pike-pole and kidding me. Where's your dog, dog man? You and he have followed me. I will kill you both and then slide you onto the rails.' " The dog creeps up from behind and catches Paul by the throat with "a side snap of his head":

> "It was really a very neat job, considering. The Pere Marquette Resort Limited removed all the traces. So, you see, when you said that Paul Black Bird was drunk and lay down on the Pere Marquette tracks you weren't quite right. That Indian couldn't get drunk. He only got crazy on drink."

8

Except for a little too much stage business and tobacco, the story is vivid, believable, and extremely concise. It is, furthermore, an unusual and pleasing study of character, as the pipe-smoking, humorous, kindly Indian contrasts ironically with his murderous experiences. The young Hemingway's desire to shock the class with drink and mayhem combines with the truer aim to reproduce the Indian's simple character and speech: " 'Yes. He was a bad Indian. Up on the upper peninsula he couldn't get drunk. He used to drink all day—everything. But he couldn't get drunk. Then he would go crazy; but he wasn't drunk. He was crazy because he couldn't get drunk.' " This is Hemingway's iterative prose suddenly full grown, and actually more cogent than that in a familiar passage in *The Sun Also Rises* (after a little too much Gertrude Stein): "Mike was a bad drunk. Brett was a good drunk. Bill was a good drunk. Cohn was never drunk. Mike was unpleasant after he passed a certain point." Hemingway is still using drink to shock propriety, with all the adolescent's theatrical expertise in the precise shades of sin. "Sepi Jingan" opened a significant subject for Hemingway, in the first exploration of which he found his characteristic simple and repetitive style.

But Oak Park was to turn the stylist toward a profession, too. His high-school popularity depended more than anything on his columns in imitation of the tremendously popular Ring Lardner of the Chicago *Tribune*. Hemingway was later to inscribe a book "To Ring Lardner from his early imitator and always admirer, Ernest Hemingway." His imitations actually contributed little to his style, except by way of exercise and ease, but they did strongly cast him in the role of journalist. In his high-school columns he is writing about himself, boldly and colloquially—as indeed he continues to do, in disguise, throughout his work. He writes to his sister, editor for the week: "The *Trapeze* is short of stuff and so don't get sore if I string this out because anyway you should give me lots of space because we are sisters and brothers." He announces a fictitious dinner dance: "Messers Morris Musselman, Fred Wilcoxen, Ernest Hemingway, Abraham Lincoln and General Joffre will not be among those present, all having perfect alibis." And a new anti-prohibition party: "Its leaders, led by Tom Cusack, nominated the modest editor of these columns and announced their slogan as 'Hemingway and a full Stein.' "

His work on the school paper led to the Kansas City *Star* in the fall of 1917, a family solution to Hemingway's wanting to enlist

9

after graduation. The *Star* put a finish on his style and gave him a profession in which he could adventurously escape society while he served it, and could observe life while he lived it, an exile by profession.

KANSAS CITY

As Charles Fenton tells us in *The Apprenticeship of Ernest Hemingway*, the typical newspaperman on the Kansas City *Star* was a hardworking, literate journalist with a pride in meticulous prose and a novel in manuscript. C. G. Wellington, assistant city editor, directly responsible for the quality of the *Star*'s prose, won Hemingway's admiration: "Pete Wellington was a stern disciplinarian, very just and very harsh, and I can never say properly how grateful I am to have worked under him." The *Star*'s style sheet was a perfect Hemingway handbook, emphasizing qualities he had already discovered in high school: "Use short sentences. Use short first paragraphs. Use vigorous English. Be positive, not negative. Avoid the use of adjectives, especially such extravagant ones as *splendid, gorgeous, grand, magnificent, etc.*" The rules demanded fresh language and economy. "Those were the best rules I ever learned for the business of writing," Hemingway said in 1940. "I've never forgotten them. No man with any talent, who feels and writes truly about the thing he is trying to say, can fail to write well if he abides by them." He was "enormously excited" to learn from Wellington and the style sheet the evocative power of brevity, the prevailing quality of all his work, which he had already sensed without name or creed in his high-school stories.

To Wellington's firm direction was added the heady influence of Lionel Calhoun Moise, "a very picturesque, dynamic, big-hearted, hard-drinking and hard-fighting man," as Hemingway remembered him, one addicted to hitting cops and throwing typewriters out of windows. Moise, too, was a writer's writer, with a creed: "Pure objective writing is the only form of storytelling. . . . No stream of consciousness nonsense; no playing dumb observer one paragraph and God Almighty the next." Spare prose and the objective view— these were the lessons of Kansas City.

Furthermore, the *Star* specialized in short narrative news stories of one and two paragraphs, printing as many as twenty-five on the front page. Hemingway took great pains with these. They are exactly the kind of compact noncommittal sketch that was to illuminate his foreign correspondence and to make up his little Paris volume, *in our time* (1924)—two sketches of which come straight from Kansas City.

Hemingway's seven months as an eighteen-year-old cub on the *Star* were enthusiastic ones. He is remembered as always riding with the police or disappearing into an ambulance. His beat was made to order: blood and crime and "some shady characters I got to know." He was living directly between vivid experience and his typewriter. "When I get a little excited this damn type mill goes haywire on me," he explained to a new boy awed by his key-jamming furor in the newsroom. He was seeing journalism as his unusually literary seniors were seeing it, as a way both to be and to become a writer. He talked into the night about his work, and declared, as they did, that he would write the great American novel.

ITALY

The new boy in the newsroom was Theodore B. Brumback, just returned, in November, 1917, from driving an ambulance in France. Brumback had been ineligible for the army because of a blind eye; Hemingway had been rejected twelve times because of poor vision in an eye apparently weak from birth and perhaps further damaged in boxing at the Chicago gym. When, next spring, a news-service story described the need for ambulance drivers in Italy, Brumback and Hemingway cabled applications before the item got to press. On April 30, 1918, they left the *Star* for some fishing with two other newspaper friends at the Hemingway summer home in Michigan. Two weeks later, their orders arrived. They left for New York in their fishing clothes. On May 12, as "provisional acting second lieutenants" in the Red Cross, they marched down Fifth Avenue in review before President Wilson. Brumback described Hemingway as "delirious with excitement."

In Italy, he soon tired of driving ambulances in a quiet sector. He transferred farther east to Red Cross canteen duty at the village of Fossalta on the Piave River, where an Italian offensive was under way. Still too far from action, he wheedled permission to take chocolate, tobacco, and postcards directly into the trenches, riding up laden with them on his bicycle. So, for six days, he could see the action he craved.

But, at midnight on July 8, 1918, Hemingway, in Italy scarcely a month, two weeks short of his nineteenth birthday, was hit by a mortar shell while handing out chocolate to Italian soldiers. According to Theodore Brumback's letter to the Hemingways, the earliest report, the man standing between Hemingway and the explosion was killed, and another lost both legs. Hemingway, having regained consciousness, carried a third man on his back to the dressing station. He remembered nothing of it. He had taken two hundred and twenty-seven steel fragments, plus one machine gun bullet, mostly in one leg.

For the next three months at the Red Cross Hospital in Milan, undergoing twelve operations, Hemingway wrote stories remembered by his ambulance friend Bill Horne as very good, ones apparently never to appear in print, though sent around to the publishers by a friend in Chicago. The wounding, the soul that seemed to be sliding away "like you'd pull a silk handerkerchief out of a pocket by one corner," the feet that felt like boots full of hot water, the trip by stretcher, which was often dropped, along a road under shellfire, the two-hour wait in a stable for an ambulance, the pain and terror, had opened a deep compulsion to write. Hemingway also fell in love with Agnes von Kurowsky, an American Red Cross nurse, who was to contribute to the characterization of the British Brett Ashley, and virtually to become the Scottish Catherine Barkley.

But Hemingway never went back to the front, as his fiction has encouraged us to believe. Brumback's letter of October 5, 1918, mentions the hope of Hemingway's release from the hospital "in a couple of weeks." The Armistice came on November 11, 1918; an interview in the Chicago *Evening American,* January 21, 1919, tells of Hemingway's landing as a convalescent in New York, "the worst shot-up man that had come home from the war area." He went back to Oak Park, a nineteen-year-old hero with a cane, in a uniform pieced together to his own fancy: a tunic traded from one man, a black leather coat from a dead friend, and shirt and boots bought at Gibraltar. He showed the perforated pants of his wounding to the assembled students of Oak Park High. Two years later the Italian government presented him in a ceremony at Chicago its silver medal of valor with cross of merit inscribed "Tenente Ernesto Hemingway."

CORRESPONDENT AT LARGE

War is the writer's greatest experience, Hemingway has asserted. It was so, with him. His friend Bill Horne has said, "Hemingway, to my own certain knowledge, never threw off his experiences in the war." The buried uncertainty evident throughout his life was torn open, never quite to heal, always to haunt and urge his creative imagination. He spent the summer of 1919 with his family at the summer home on Walloon Lake, then stayed on alone into the winter, nearly freezing, writing stories, starting a novel, healing his wounds, confident of being able to make a living by writing fiction. Before the end of the year, he was on the staff of the Toronto *Star Weekly,* the Saturday supplement of the *Daily Star,* for which he was also to write during the next four years, energetic but still unsure, irritating his new friends by constantly shadow-boxing as he talked or listened.

Hemingway wrote thousands of words for the Toronto *Star,* beginning with features on the outdoors and ending with competent foreign correspondence—at the ages of twenty-two and twenty-three and twenty-four. His writing became more fluid; he interviewed Mussolini and Clemenceau; he covered diplomatic conferences and the unfolding events of Europe. In Asia Minor, he saw the Greco-Turkish war of 1922, where, he claimed, he "really learned about war." Seasoned, sharp, politically wise, his writing continued to be nearly narrative—first-person accounts of Europe vivified with vignettes and with short dialogues: Mussolini garish in black shirt and white spats; inflation in the Ruhr, in the remarks of a waiter. He wrote very few routine news stories. He was writing history as immediate experience: "All day I have been passing them, dirty, tired, unshaven, wind-bitten soldiers . . ."; "I saw . . ."; "I asked. . . ." He is at the scene, observing for his Canadian readers. This is Ernest Hemingway of the by-line speaking, even when the "I" is out of sight: "There were strings of German hikers . . ."; "It looked peaceful . . ."; "It was a nice morning." He is assured and mature. He is economizing his thoughts for the cablegram ("read the cabelese, only the cabelese; isn't it a great language?") and filling in detail for the wordage and the pocketbook. To create his mature fiction he will need only to change the "I" into Nick or Jake Barnes or Lieutenant Henry and to make his economy wholly literary.

The journalist had, in fact, begun to threaten the writer. In Kansas City the two had seemed synonymous. He had kept at his fiction diligently and unsuccessfully in Toronto. From the fall of 1920 to the fall of 1921 he was in Chicago working as associate editor of *Co-operative Commonwealth,* a pious organ of a co-operative movement that turned out, to Hemingway's disillusionment, to be a fraud. Hemingway wrote feature and editorial copy, with a good deal of the biblical phrasing and allusion required by the management. His stylistic use of the Bible and his contempt for commerce were mutually strengthened. And the antagonism between journalism and "writing" grew.

Hemingway had been living in the spacious apartment of the Y. K. Smiths, along with Bill Horne, now in advertising, whose apartment he had previously been sharing. Smith, also an advertising man, was generous and fatherly, an old friend of the Horton's Bay vacations whom Hemingway had known from the age of twelve (Smith's son Bill is certainly the prototype for Nick's friend Bill in *In Our Time,* with perhaps something of Bill Horne mixed in). The apartment contained another young ad man (out of work) and two young ladies: Smith's sister, Katherine, who was to marry John Dos Passos, and a free-lance-writer friend of hers. The apartment was literate and lively. There Hemingway met Hadley Richardson, beautiful, red-haired, eight years his senior, and a friend of Katherine Smith's from St. Louis. And there he also met Sherwood Anderson, whose work he had avidly admired and whom he claimed as model and was to deny as master. Anderson, more than anything, represented the writer who had broken with the workaday world to write and to succeed.

Hemingway married Hadley at Horton's Bay on September 3, 1921, and left with his bride for Paris on December 8, as "roving correspondent for the *Star,* with headquarters in Paris." Anderson had sent them off with a sheaf of enthusiastic letters of introduction, notably one to Gertrude Stein. Stein urged him to give up journalism. From Anderson, Hemingway learned to see his own central subject: loneliness against the world. From Stein, he learned to polish what he had had from the first: economy, understatement, and a repetition that amplifies and resonates his meaning. He had always worked hard. While the Smith apartment had chatted, Hemingway had been in his room at his typewriter, trying to get down the smells of Kid Howard's gym, having systematically taken them in, earlier in the evening. "You've got to see it, feel it, smell it, hear it," he had told the Smith apartment. "I always worked by myself, years before I met Ezra or Gertrude." The mature writers merely confirmed and encouraged the strength in his talent.

Gertrude Stein, however, also gave him a conscious approach. From her, for the first time, he learned that writing was a matter of rewriting. His hard work before had all been additive, trying new things, trying another story. He showed her the incipient novel. She told him to condense, to start all over again, to prune his description. She told him to see as a painter sees, Cézanne in particular, and then Goya. His frequent emphasis on "country" owes much to Stein: he writes to her of his "Big Two-Hearted River" in her own terms, ". . . I'm trying to do the country like Cézanne . . . the country is swell, I made it all up, so I see it all and part of it comes out the way it ought to, . . . but isn't writing a hard job though?" He had not, in fact, "made the country up" at all. He is writing with fair accuracy of the country around Seney, Michigan. But he seems to mean what Stein means: that the writer must re-create the image in his mind before he can make it real on paper.

Stein, along with Ezra Pound (with whom he was soon boxing), apparently had also encouraged him to go on with his poetry. Hemingway, continually battered by rejections since 1918, had finally, in May, 1922, landed a short and tasteless satirical prose fantasy ("A Divine Gesture") in *The Double Dealer,* "A National Magazine from the South, published at New Orleans." His friendship with Anderson had helped. Among the contributors were Djuna Barnes, Edmund Wilson, Allen Tate, Hart Crane, and Pound: "Ernest M. Hemingway is a young American writer who lives in Paris and enjoys the favor of Ezra Pound. He expects shortly to bring out a book of poems." The next issue contained "Ultimately," Hemingway's first poem in public print:

> He tried to spit out the truth;
> Dry mouthed at first,
> He drooled and slobbered in the end;
> Truth dribbling his chin.

As Young notes, "Ultimately" suggests the manner of Stephen Crane, on whom Hemingway is to draw more profitably for "The Short Happy Life of Francis Macomber," and perhaps for Lieutenant Henry. But, for better or worse, in "Ultimately" Hemingway is un-covering the metaphor in a colloquial phrase ("spit out"), and he is recording the writer's dilemma of too little and too much, as he works at what Hemingway has repeatedly stated as his central aim, to "write truly." But "Ultimately" is perhaps more interesting in that it fills out what must be one of the most important pages among modern literary curiosa: above it, and dominating the page, is "Portrait" by William Faulkner, six Eliotic, mannered, but lovely stanzas of iambic pentameter—the two giants of American prose together as fledgling poets. Faulkner was to reprint "Ultimately" on the back cover of his *Salmagundi.*

Harriet Monroe brought out six brief Hemingway poems in *Poetry* (January, 1923) under the general heading "Wanderings." They are undistinguished, but not without craft. In "Oily Weather," Hemingway again impudently turns up a sleeping slang metaphor: the ship's "screw turns a throb." The old female sea rolls with desire, but "throbbing ships scorn it." Hemingway has suggested the sexual antithesis between male and female he had already portrayed in the yet unpublished "Up in Michigan." "Riparto d'Assalto" gives us the sex and death on the Italian front that will orchestrate into *A Farewell to Arms*. Here, Hemingway exercises his ear for repetition in the manner of Vachel Lindsay, as Young has noted. A truck load of Italian soldiers:

> Drummed their boots on the camion floor
> . . . .
> Lieutenants thought of a Mestre whore—
> Warm and soft and sleepy whore
> Cozy, warm and lovely whore

—all to be blown up at the end. Mestre is ten miles north of Venice on the way to Fossalta, where Hemingway himself had been blown up five years before. This is Hemingway's first literary rendering of his central traumatic experiences of July 8, 1918.

The disillusion of war also goes into "Champs d'Honneur," eight lines that end:

> Soldiers pitch and cough and twitch
> All the world roars red and black
> Soldiers smother in a ditch
> Choking through the whole attack.

"Mitrailiatrice," his best, brings us back to the writer at his desk, the place where he started his poetry in his high-school ballad. Like the ballad, it is a piece of writing about writing:

> The mills of the gods grind slowly:
> But this mill
> Chatters in mechanical staccato.
> Ugly short infantry of the mind,
> Advancing over difficult terrain,
> Make this Corona
> Their mitraileuse.

Aside from the avant-garde French (*mitraileuse*), the poem again shows the writer at work, seeing the metaphor in the common word.

The playful parody of high school has now become the serious twist-ing of a line from Longfellow, the schoolboy's anathema: "Though the mills of God grind slowly. . . ." The writers thoughts and fingers (*ugly short infantry*) make a machine gun (*mitraileuse*) of his typewriter. The "mitrailiatrice" is Hemingway himself, the "machine gun specialist," still the fiery typist of the Kansas City newsroom with his "damn type mill." The war-wise writer has re-turned to pagan gods as he grinds his colloquial mill in the battle of words against the unknown. Such serious, ironic parody will re-cur in Hemingway's work, especially as he reduces his Biblical touches to a kind of lower-case grimness. "Chapter Heading," an ironic commentary on prayer after frolic, was reprinted in *Best Poems of 1923*.

The "book of poems" soon to be brought out, to which *The Double Dealer* had referred, was to include this selection from *Poetry*. But an accident changed the plan. While at Lausanne, Switzerland, cov-ering the important international conference that followed the Greco-Turkish war, Hemingway had met Lincoln Steffens, who was en-thusiastic about two of his stories (apparently "Up in Michigan" and "My Old Man"). Mrs. Hemingway, coming down from Paris for Christmas, thought to bring all of Hemingway's work for Steffens to see; and all of it, the total of Hemingway's work to date, care-fully copied and arranged in folders, vanished from her compartment with a suitcase stolen before the train started from Paris. Both Hemingways were crushed, and Hemingway, in his first wife's words, probably never recovered from the pain of it. But spending some time with Ezra Pound at Rapallo, after the conference and a skiing vacation, the Hemingways met Robert McAlmon, recent publisher of Pound's first cantos. McAlmon took pity, and in the spring of 1923 he advertised *2 Stories & 10 Poems* by Hemingway.

The facts leave room for conjecture. The poems for the volume promised in *The Double Dealer* of May, 1922, must have been lost with the suitcase, except for the six in *Poetry;* and hopes for pub-lishing that volume must have vanished with the thief. But had the volume appeared, Hemingway might have continued to struggle in an alien medium and manner. Now that he had found a new publisher, he needed more copy; to make up a book, McAlmon evi-dently agreed to bring out Hemingway's extant "works," not poems only, but two stories saved from theft: "Up in Michigan," influenced by Stein but put in a drawer because she thought it too crude for publication, and "My Old Man," influenced by Anderson and saved from theft by having been out looking for a publisher. The book of poems became a book of poems and stories.

Hemingway also had written, or had on hand from recent rejections, the four additional poems to make up the volume: (1) "Oklahoma," which begins "All of the Indians are dead," and turns sexually bitter; (2) "Captives," whose exhaustion is the cure for hatred and a long campaign, and makes death easy; (3) "Montparnasse," where there are no successful suicides because of emetics, and "the people one knows can be found at the café"; and (4) "Along with Youth," with the dusty trophies of boyhood and a hint of the country from which soon is to emerge "The Big Two-Hearted River" and "Now I Lay Me." Hemingway was to go on for the next six years with occasional poems, mostly satirical, mostly terrible, particularly in the periodical *Der Querschnitt* (the "cross-section"). But the accident of 1922 and the volume of 1923 were to confirm his bent for prose.

At this time, Hemingway wrote "Out of Season," as McAlmon's change from *"2 Stories"* to *"Three Stories"* indicates. In it Hemingway moved beyond Stein and Anderson to Hemingway. Set in the Dolomite Alps, where the Hemingways were to spend more than one vacation, the story has just the understated tenderness and desolate antagonism that would have prevailed between a young couple after the loss of a valise of manuscripts. The season is exactly the season, too early for fishing, that they would have been spending in the Dolomites or with Pound after the Lausanne conference. The Italian gardener, self-proclaimed out-of-season fishing expert, is exactly the authentic comic center of inefficiency and disappointment that gives the story its core. In the mixture of Alpine languages, no one can quite understand anyone. This is real Hemingway, precise, amusing, tender, tough, undercut, implying a deep center of human frustration: the universal inability to understand, not to be alone. But the less typical though excellent "My Old Man" became Hemingway's first story to win a literary honor: inclusion in *The Best Short Stories of 1923*.

ᵉᵍ NICK—IN OUR TIME

HEMINGWAY was soon to discover Nick Adams and to produce *In Our Time,* his first and best book of stories, a counterpointing of the journalistic and the fictive, a perfect resolution of Hemingway's uncertainty between journalism and fiction, and between poetry and prose. Hemingway's year of discovery was 1923. Early spring had produced "Out of Season" and carried him into new territory; and he had seen *Three Stories and Ten Poems,* his first volume, off to the printer's. Moreover, he was writing a series of highly compact journalistic sketches, almost grim prose poems, on the pattern of the Kansas City *Star,* and he was working on "The Big Two-Hearted River." The "Exiles" number of the *Little Review* (Paris) printed the series of six sketches on April 1, 1923. And then he went to Madrid for his first bullfight, and his first experience of Spain.

In the same issue of the *Little Review* appears Hemingway's "They All Want Peace, What is Peace," a prose poem treating the Lausanne conference with the political cynicism of William Bolitho (whom he met there) and in the manner of Gertrude Stein, with whom he had lunched and talked away the afternoon before returning to Lausanne from Paris, composing his bawdy and derivative lines on the train, still somewhere between journalism and poetry.

The six *Little Review* sketches led directly to others, all to be printed as the Paris booklet *in our time* (1924) and then to be interleaved among the stories of *In Our Time* (New York, 1925). Each of the first six is a single tight paragraph: the shortest ("chapter 4") only seventy-five words; the longest ("chapter 2"), only a hundred and eighty-five. All the compression that Kansas City, Gertrude Stein, cablegrams, and practice had taught him is here—journalism crystallized into art. But something new is also evident. Three of the sketches are not objective reports at all but dramatic monologues: sharp disembodied extracts, perfectly caught, from the wartime anecdotes of others. Hemingway's dispatches had already contained short dialogues. But these new monologues return significantly to the First World War, the locus of Hemingway's imagination. The first is the voice of a Frenchman: "Everyone was drunk. The whole battery was drunk going along the road in the dark. . . ." The high-school sensationalist has found the affinity of alcohol and terror abroad in the actual world.

Hemingway is also doing what he had done in high school with his Michigan Indian and in his Toronto columns with his Belgians and Germans, what he was to do in his novels with his Italians and Spaniards—he is catching in English the quaint effects of foreign speech: "The lieutenant kept riding his horse out into the fields and saying to him, 'I'm drunk, I tell you, mon vieux. Oh, I am so soused.'" And the unknown French soldier's voice continues like that of a disembodied soul: "It was funny going along that road. That was when I was a kitchen Corporal." Hemingway is discovering what Dante had found and what Eliot had recently recaptured in his *Waste Land*.

The other two monologues are lighter: transcriptions from the tailored British ironics of Hemingway's friend, Captain Eric Edward Dorman-Smith of His Majesty's Fifth Fusiliers. In others, the dramatic monologue fades. "Chapter 2" is the voice of America but it is not the voice of the American whom Hemingway depicts in his bullfighting articles for the Toronto *Star Weekly* in October, as Fenton has reasonably conjectured. Hemingway had as yet neither visited Spain nor seen a bullfight. As with the British sketches, he is retelling a friend's anecdote, that of Henry ("Mike") Strater, who painted three portraits of Hemingway (1922, 1923, 1930): "From my stories about Spain," Mr. Strater writes in a letter to me, August 18, 1962, "Hem wrote his first bull-fight story (about the Kid) before he had ever been to Spain. I did not like Bull-fights, to me they are tawdry." For republication in *in our time*, Hemingway deleted some of the slang in his version of Strater's anecdote, turning away from the speaker to the imagined fight itself.

In "chapter 6" the speaker's voice has merged with the author's. Shorty Wornall, a newsreel cameraman, had told Hemingway about six Greek cabinet ministers executed by firing squad on November 28, 1922. Hemingway has exhibited Wornall's idiom elsewhere: "Got some swell shots of a burning village to-day. . . . Good show. . . ." But here Hemingway concentrates entirely on the event, in his own tight authorial prose. (Charles Fenton somehow detects Wornall's voice here and takes the opposite view.) This is the only one of the six *Little Review* sketches that did not undergo revision.

"Chapter 3" is probably the best, coming straight from Hemingway's own reporting, catching the French corporal's dreary voice in Hemingway's own. It is a thorough reworking, as Fenton has shown, of an October cablegram from Thrace. "Minarets stuck up in the rain" it begins; and it ends: "It rained all through the evacuation." Hemingway's conjunction of rain and misery begins here, as Carlos Baker notes. Furthermore, both the cablegram and the sketch end with a woman in labor in a cart in the rain, a blanket held over her, a little girl looking on in horror. Birth and death were to become themes of *In Our Time;* and *A Farewell to Arms* was to complete the orchestration of dark rain and childbirth and death.

In the twelve sketches added to complete *in our time,* Hemingway moves still closer to the short story and to his primary material. Three remain largely journalistic, to be sure. The last, about the deposed King George of Greece, is again taken second hand from Wornall; two are anecdotes from Kansas City. But Hemingway adds to his first bullfighting sketch ("chapter 2") five more in direct succession ("chapters 12" through "16"). Moreover, two—also in direct succession, as if episodes in the same story—are sketches of Maera, a real fighter; but the last of these is patently fictionalized. Maera was alive, though dying of consumption, when Hemingway wrote in mid-1923, but Hemingway imagines how Maera feels as he is gored and then dies on the operating table, a step from objective journalism clear into subjective fiction, and with the same Maera he was to fictionalize superbly in "The Undefeated." Nine of the sketches move beyond Hemingway's original one-paragraph limit; two of these are promoted to short stories in *In Our Time.* "Chapter 10" ("A Very Short Story") is a love affair between a wounded American soldier and a British nurse in Milan (Padua in *In Our Time*), a fictionalization of Hemingway's own unhappy wartime romance and the seed of *A Farewell to Arms.*

And in the first of the new group ("chapter 7"), we encounter Nick. He has no surname yet. He is wounded in the spine and propped against a church, a wounded Italian friend named Rinaldi lying face down beside him. In further stories, Nick will become Nick Adams, with wounds in legs instead of spine. Rinaldi will become the doctor friend of Lieutenant Henry in *A Farewell to Arms.* Another sketch tells of terror under bombardment at Fossalta. Hemingway has moved from journalism and secondhand reports into his own painful experiences.

Hemingway probably wrote the twelve additional *in our time* sketches between early March, when the first six would have had to go to the printer, and mid-July, when he delivered the manuscript to William Bird's Three Mountains Press. Ever since the previous summer, in 1922, Bird and Ezra Pound had talked of including Hemingway in their series of contemporary booklets. And even though Hemingway delivered his copy almost as *Three Stories and Ten Poems* was being issued, he apparently expected the short booklet to beat the book into print. But Bird was printing by hand on handmade paper, and others were ahead of Hemingway: *in our time* —170 copies—appeared in the spring of 1924, the sixth and last of a series that included Pound's *Indiscretions,* Ford Madox Ford's *Women and Men,* and William Carlos Williams' *The Great American Novel.* The cover was a montage of newspaper headlines and clippings, suggesting the journalistic jumble "in our time." And dead center on the scrambled clippings, as on each book in the series, was the signet of the Three Mountains Press: a small rectangle the shape of a book, containing three simple lines, representing mountains, and the motto: "Levavi oculos meos in montes," the beginning of the one hundred twenty-first psalm, in Latin dress, suiting the iconoclastic irony of the Poundian group and enforcing the Biblical irony in Hemingway's title.

Hemingway's was the only booklet of the series with title in lower case. Perhaps Bird was copying the new *transatlantic review,* started by Ford in January, 1924, of which Hemingway was associate editor. The April issue reviewed *in our time* favorably. This issue also printed part of Gertrude Stein's *The Making of Americans,* which Hemingway had gotten for the magazine, and which he had copied out from Miss Stein's manuscript and edited—hence her claim that Hemingway's handling of her copy had taught him how to write. But more important, the "Work in Progress" section of this *transatlantic*—along with a piece by Tristan Tzara and a piece of Joyce's *Finnegans Wake*—contained an untitled story by Hemingway. This was "Indian Camp," Hemingway's first complete story about Nick, the story Hemingway was to place first in *In Our Time,* to be published the next year in New York by Boni and Liveright (October 5, 1925).

Hemingway's reputation had been spreading. Edmund Wilson had shown Hemingway's work to F. Scott Fitzgerald. Fitzgerald had urged Maxwell Perkins of Scribner's to publish him. Donald Ogden Stewart was urging the same to the Doran company, as were Sherwood Anderson and Harold Loeb to Boni and Liveright, with Loeb actually rescuing the manuscript from rejection. Liveright cabled an offer; Hemingway accepted by return cable, as requested. Ten days later came a letter of inquiry from Scribner's, whom Hemingway would have preferred, since Anderson and Boni and Liveright seemed to be waning. But soon Liveright's sensible rejection of *The Torrents of Spring* was to release Hemingway from his contract, and Hemingway's marriage with Scribner's was solemnized.

The public evolution of *In Our Time* had continued rapidly. Soon after "Indian Camp," the *transatlantic* published "The Doctor and the Doctor's Wife" (December, 1924), another story of Nick's boyhood. Next month came "Cross Country Snow," in which Nick gets the name of Adams. Simultaneously, the *Little Review* was printing "Mr. and Mrs. Elliot." In the spring of 1925, *Contact Collection of Contemporary Writers* included "Soldier's Home," and *This Quarter* (Paris, May, 1925) published "The Big Two-Hearted River."

Other works also were appearing: short articles for *transatlantic* and *This Quarter;* "The Undefeated," to be published in French, German, and English magazines; and a final rash of poems, sent for Hemingway by a Paris friend to *Der Querschnitt*. One can see how, in the foreign language of a rising writer, the poems might appeal to an experimental German editor. One cannot see how Hemingway and his friends could think them good even as jokes. "The Age Demanded" and "The Earnest Liberal's Lament" are passable sophomorics. But "The Soul of Spain with McAlmon and Bird the Publishers, Parts I–VI" runs mostly like this:

PART IV of the same story
After a while there were no bullfights. What the hell no bullfights? No bullfights. No you really can't mean it no bullfights. But there were no bullfights.

PART V follows
We got on the train and went somewhere else.

"The Lady Poets with Footnotes," also a series of prose statements, begins with "One lady poet was a nymphomaniac and wrote for Vanity Fair" and ends with a footnote on the lady poet who was "big and fat and no fool," informing the public that "she smoked cigars all right, but her stuff was no good": Amy Lowell, in short, and in grandstanding acrimony.

But "The Soul of Spain" (Part I), "in the manner of Gertrude Stein," wins the prize for being sophomoric and gratuitously offensive. It begins:

> In the rain in the rain in the rain in the rain in Spain
> Does it rain in Spain?
> Oh yes my dear on the contrary and there are no bullfights.

Innocent and amusing enough. But then Hemingway proceeds, through a long, anal bacchanalia about Home, Democracy, Relativity, Dictators, and Mencken, to build a fecal monument to Ezra Pound. It is a remarkable performance. E. E. Cummings at about the same time was wonderfully committing a similar nuisance in his "Poem, or Beauty Hurts Mr. Vinal" (Harold Vinal, editor of *Voices,* who had appeared with Hemingway in *The Double Dealer*), but doing it with irresistible satirical wit. Such was simply beyond Hemingway. The intense creative strain behind *In Our Time* seems to have demanded a lower vent, a satirical attack on friends, or former friends, such as *The Torrents of Spring* was to make in recuperation from *The Sun Also Rises.*

❧ ☙

But the effort to record the smells of Kid Howard's gym had continued in Hemingway's prose until it produced *In Our Time,* as he was later to testify in *Death in the Afternoon:*

> I was trying to write then and I found the greatest difficulty, aside from knowing truly what you really felt, rather than what you were supposed to feel, and had been taught to feel, was to put down what really happened in action; what the actual things were which produced the emotion that you experienced. In writing for a newspaper you told what happened and, with one trick and another, you communicated the emotion aided by the element of timeliness which gives a certain emotion to any account of something that has happened on that day; but the real thing, the sequence of motion and fact which made the emotion and which would be as valid in a year or in ten years or, with luck and if you stated it purely enough, always, was beyond me and I was working very hard to try to get it. The only place where you could see life and death, i.e., violent death now that the wars were over, was in the bull ring and I wanted very much to go to Spain where I could study it. I was trying to learn to write, commencing with the simplest things, and one of the simplest things of all and the most fundamental is violent death.

This is the program that produced *In Our Time,* first the sketches, then the book. Hemingway did go to Spain, taking a vacation from "The Big Two-Hearted River."

The program shows both Hemingway's dedication and his moral uncertainty. It is difficult to "know truly what you really felt" because what you "had been taught to feel" must necessarily be false—so runs the Hemingway fallacy, the formula of youthful rebellion. Fortunately, Hemingway's creative perception is better than his theoretical explanation of it, as formulated later in *Death in the Afternoon*. In the stories and sketches of *In Our Time*, he attended to the experience and spectacle of death without degenerating into the sadistic connoisseurship his theory suggests. He is able to catch the old moral truths, either taught or discovered, about the rightness of man's bravery and constancy and dedication and about the wrongness of man's cruelty, indifference, selfishness, and pettiness, and even the tragic wrongness of death itself, which ends this life of values and potential. He gets them as Goya got them, even though he understands no more than that Goya had "made death permanent": "But in the case of an execution by a firing squad, or a hanging . . . if these very simple things were to be made permanent, as, say, Goya tried to make them in *Los Desastros de la Guerra,* it could not be done with any shutting of the eyes." He wanted to study these things, he says, as one cannot when writing "immediately after for the first edition of an afternoon newspaper."

In *In Our Time* Hemingway studies the disasters of war, particularly as they culminate in the disillusion and psychic crippling of Nick Adams. The timeliness of journalism still "gives a certain emotion." These are stories "in our time," with a journalistic sprinkle of sketches—taking a phrase Hemingway used often: "It was nice to see a great writer in our time" (of Joyce); ". . . the very finest poetry of our time" (of Yeats), a phrase frequently and ironically on Colonel Cantwell's lips. For his book, Hemingway is also reviving the original implication from the service of Evening Prayer, making it somber and ironic: we get not peace in our time, O Lord, even after war (as the Lausanne conference had taught him); we get either violence or coma. Five years later (1930), Hemingway added an introductory sketch about how Greek troops, evacuating Smyrna, had broken their horses' forelegs to drown them in shallow water, events about which the narrator continues to dream —a true introduction, as Young points out in his *Ernest Hemingway,* to the horror that continued to haunt Hemingway and his sleepless heroes.

Seven of the fourteen stories are about Nick Adams, plus the central sketch of the wounded Nick, propped against the church wall

—exactly in the middle of a book, with a story of Nick at beginning and end. And we should perhaps also count the Fossalta sketch and the love story of the nameless soldier, unless we should prefer to name him Frederic Henry. The diversity of the sketches allows the book to accommodate the non-Nick stories without damaging the sequential study of Nick. The book is indeed a kind of phantom novel about Nick (as D. H. Lawrence, reviewing the book, was the first to note), with only the intense moments showing through other scattered moments in other lives. Calling the sketches "chapters," so that each "chapter" contains a sketch followed by a story, aids the novelistic impression, a lucky bonus from the rambunctious irony of calling the tiny sketches "chapters" in the first *in our time*. The book has remarkable unity, a consistently grim and attractive sadness, even from the brighter pieces, among the stark scatter of journalism, its air of timeliness giving a certain emotion.

In a letter to Edmund Wilson, October 18, 1924, Hemingway describes his intention:

> Finished the book of 14 stories with a chapter of *In Our Time* [i.e., *in our time*] between each story—that is the way they were meant to go—to give the picture of the whole between examining it in detail. Like looking with your eyes at something, say a passing coastline, and then looking at it with 15X binoculars. Or rather, maybe, looking at it and then going in and living in it—and then coming out and looking at it again.
>
> . . . I think you would like it, it has a pretty good unity.

Of course, the book is uneven. "Mr. and Mrs. Elliot" and "The Revolutionist" (formerly "chapter 11" of *in our time*) are negligible. "Cat in the Rain" does not equal the fine "Out of Season," to which it now becomes a good feminine companion study, the only story in the book from the woman's viewpoint, and one of Hemingway's only two (the other is "Up in Michigan"). The remaining two non-Nick stories are frequently anthologized.

"My Old Man," reprinted from *Three Stories and Ten Poems,* with its debt to Anderson's "I Want to Know Why" (howsoever indirect, and denied by Hemingway), is nevertheless a fine story, Hemingway's only one in what might be called "the first person innocent." It is told by a boy, son of a crooked American jockey in Europe who is killed (in a black cap and a black jacket with a white cross on it) when he buys a horse and tries to go straight. The little aging jockey, pathetically good as a father and bad as a man, is superb. The boy's idiom exactly conveys the irony of his imperceptions and his heartbreak. The boy's description of Kzar is probably that of an actual horse Hemingway mentions in *Death in the Afternoon* along with a "classic steeplechase race at Auteuil," like the one in the story.

"Soldier's Home," too, is derivative, and good. It begins with a touch from Fitzgerald, with the hero in snapshots, and continues with a Steinish string of he-liked-he-liked, at first sounding like an exercise in repetition. But soon the exercise becomes, as it were, the repetitive disillusioned mind of Krebs. In the war, he had been brave a number of times, doing "the only thing for a man to do, easily and naturally, when he might have done something else. . . ." Thinking of these times used to make him "feel cool and clear inside," but now, back home, the feeling and then the events themselves are lost to him. No one will listen to the war as it was. Everything in society and in his Methodist home seems false. He cannot get interested in a nice girl, as his mother wishes: Krebs is experiencing the characteristic Hemingway emotional impotence, since nice girls represent conventional falsity and emotional commitment. Krebs wants only for his "life to go smoothly." For the moment he will go over to the school and watch his kid sister play softball.

"Soldier's Home" is a preliminary study of the war-shocked or shell-shocked state of mind portrayed in "The Big Two-Hearted River," published immediately after. Krebs, the young Methodist who can't pray, damaged by war though brave and unwounded, now becomes Nick Adams (first wounded and propped against a defunct church) trying to get away and live smoothly for a moment by fishing in upper Michigan. In *In Our Time,* the study of Nick Adams progresses directly from "Indian Camp" to "The Big Two-Hearted River," from first story to last. The Nick of "Cross Country Snow," with pregnant wife and circumstances almost contemporaneous with Hemingway's as he wrote it, is factually inconsistent with the bachelor of the other stories. In *The Autobiography of Alice B. Toklas,* Gertrude Stein gives evidence of how close to Hemingway the story must have been: ". . . then all of a sudden he announced that his wife was enceinte and then with great bitterness, and I, I am too young to be a father." But the story catches the central appeal of the youthful masculine world, the downhill sweep on skis, with a bad leg from the war and female convention and responsibility as reminders that it cannot last. It is a clear and flawless story.

Childbirth and death—these themes emanate from the sketches, and "Indian Camp" initiates the reader with perhaps the most appalling birth-death story ever written. Nick's doctor-father delivers an Indian baby without anesthetic by "Caesarian with a jack-knife . . . sewing it up with nine-foot, tapered gut leaders." And the baby's father, in the upper bunk with an ax wound in the foot, is found to have cut his throat with a razor during the operation. "He couldn't stand things, I guess." The story is really about the question of endurance, the question of suicide, and the relationship of father to son. It is now startling as an ironic prognostication on future birth and suicides among the Hemingways, fathers and sons. When writing *A Farewell to Arms,* Hemingway reports that "my second son Patrick was delivered in Kansas City by Caesarian section, and while I was rewriting my father killed himself in Oak Park, Illinois. . . ." The Indian son, too, had been born through the mother's agony and the father's suicide.

But Nick is still sound enough to sustain the shock with which the father, in his short-sighted surgical confidence, has afflicted him. He has leaned back against his father with perfect confidence in the middle of the night at the beginning of the story; the relationship is still untouched at the end. The sun is rising; a bass jumps; the water feels warm: "In the early morning on the lake sitting in the stern of the boat with his father rowing, he felt quite sure that he would never die." But Nick has seen the horrible operation and the suicide's nearly severed head; and he has seen Uncle George's anger at his father's callousness.

"The Doctor and the Doctor's Wife" continues the study of the father, now named an unflattering "Henry." That this would make him "Henry Adams," a Bostonian man of letters, when Nick was to acquire a last name in the next month, seems to make little difference. Hemingway seems not to have noticed: the doctor's full name never appears in print; indeed, he is never named again. But Hemingway seems to see "Henry" as effeminate—it is heard on the lips of the doctor's wife—a name, like Dr. Hemingway's actual Clarence and his son's actual Ernest, that calls for masculine proof. It is certainly not the he-man "Nick" or "Jake" of Hemingway's first heroes. The doctor's wife is an exacting hypochondriac; the doctor has backed down from a fight with a hired Indian; and the wife's ladylike misunderstanding is the last straw. The doctor and Nick go off together to look for black squirrels, leaving the angry world and feminine propriety behind. The companionship of father and son is still intact. Nick has not seen his father's humiliation.

Hemingway, though taking out some resentment on his real father, presents the doctor with sympathy. Billy Tabeshaw of Hemingway's high-school story reappears, representing a quiet decency consistent with the first portrait. As Leicester Hemingway discloses, both Billy Tabeshaw and Dick Boulton, of the same story, were actual men, put into fiction under their actual names.

The next two stories give the growing pains of male companionship. In "The End of Something" Nick breaks off his affair with his waitress sweetheart and fishing companion; in "The Three Day Blow" he competes at literary knowledge and whisky with his friend Bill, still with the optimism of youth that can, like a hike in the wind, blow out the pain of love and keep the next time possible—all humorously and affectionately and beautifully observed.

But "The Battler" is more artistic still. Nick, knocked off a freight by the brakeman, lands on the track in the dark and in the midst of Michigan swamp. He comes upon a fire, an ex-lightweight, and a maternally protective Negro attendant. Young finds the relationship homosexual, a further shock in Nick's traumatic education. But here is another Nigger Jim, as Young perceives; and other readers may see again, in Ad and Bugs, Twain's decent companionship of outcasts (roughened for the twentieth century), and may further see that Nick is excluded even from the outcasts' firelight, as he moves off, alone, into outer darkness, up the track that connects the battering world. Warm human concern is somewhere off the main line, in the dark, in the middle of a swamp, but somewhere. Perhaps the lesson is not so bleak as Young would make it, as Nick moves out of the dark, into the light, and back into the dark again, with a warm sandwich in his pocket.

The character of Ad Francis seems to derive from lightweight champion Adolph Wolgast of Cadillac, Michigan, in his prime from 1908 to 1912, but still fighting when Hemingway was in high school, hence a part of the lore from the Chicago gym. Hemingway's hobo setting may have been transplanted from anecdotes about Stanley Ketchel, a prizefighter Hemingway mentions together with Wolgast in "The Light of the World." Hemingway had probably learned both of hobo life and of Ketchel, a former hobo, from Lionel Calhoun Moise, his Kansas City idol; according to Fenton, Hemingway had taken over Moise's hobo experiences as his own, to impress his Canadian associates, in a fabrication not unusual with Hemingway. "The Battler" makes it all honest, by fiction.

After "The Battler," we turn the page to find Nick propped against the church. But perhaps we should now fill in Nick's earlier biography, as Hemingway was to fill it in with three later stories. In "The Killers" (in *Men Without Women,* 1927)—a story much praised, one derived from Hemingway's newspaper days—Nick seems at first almost a literary accident. But the story, in an odd shift, switches to Nick's viewpoint halfway through, allowing the reader to experience with him the spectacle of a man listlessly awaiting gangland assassination. Nick is more sensitive than the others. It is he who must "get out of this town" because he "can't stand" thinking about the listless acceptance and the doom. "Ten Indians" (in *Men Without Women,* 1927) goes back to the lesser pain of adolescent jealousy and shows the first slight strain between father and son over the problem of sex. Mention again of Billy Tabeshaw along with Indians drunk in the road on the Fourth of July indicates how long some of the material had lain in Hemingway's mind.

"The Light of the World" (in *Winner Take Nothing,* 1933) concerns a seventeen-year-old "I" and a nineteen-year-old Tommy drifting through what is probably Boyne City, Michigan (it smells of tan bark, and Nick in "Fathers and Sons" is to remember the "tannery at Boyne City"). The seventeen-year-old is probably Nick, but the story cannot well be seen as another prewar bruising, as several have seen it. Ironic, grotesque, amusing, blasphemous, taking the "light of the world" to be not Christ but masculine sexuality, it is nevertheless affirmative. Steve Ketchel, a prizefighter, is the dead messiah whose "own father shot and killed him" (God, sending His Son to his death in the world), who was "like a god" and "white and clean and beautiful and smooth and fast like a tiger or like lightning." But this is the glamorized gospel. A mountainous prostitute of 350 pounds has Ketchel's true word: "You are a lovely piece, Alice." She alone has the true religion: "I'm clean and you know it and men like me, even though I'm big, and you know it, and I never lie and you know it." The listening Nick sees the light: she had "about the prettiest face I ever saw" and "a nice smooth skin and a lovely voice and she was nice all right and really friendly." His friend pulls him along. They fire a parting shot at an effeminate cook and leave, confirmed in the masculinity they are merely showing off as the story begins. Again Nick is more sensitive, more perceptive, more decent—even as he sees the "light"—than his friend.

As we have seen, Ketchel, like Wolgast, was an actual person. Jack Johnson, a Negro, did beat him, as Hemingway says (at Colma, California, October 16, 1909, in the twelfth round). He was born in Michigan (September 14, 1887), but at Grand Rapids, not Cadillac, which was Wolgast's birthplace. His name was Stanley, not Steve (Hemingway's elevation in masculinity). He was Polish (originally Stanislaus Kiecal), hence perhaps distinctly "white," as the story has him, in perfect affinity with the worshiping blonds. According to Alexander Johnston (*Ten—and Out*, New York, 1947), he was a good boxer but was also noted for a "flaming offense" and "berserk fury," which makes him exactly the cleanly tiger the story records. He had run away to the hobo jungles as a boy, learning to fight to survive. He was a great reader. He was shot to death, not by his father, as Hemingway's Christian diagram requires, but by "one of his own farm-hands after a quarrel over a girl," at Conway, Missouri, October 16, 1910. All of this, four or five years before the Chicago gym, eight years before Kansas City, would have become glorious anecdote by the time young Hemingway arrived.

Now we are ready for Nick at a later date, as we turn from "The Battler" (and its background) to the first sketch of Nick. Here is the wounded soldier resting against the wall of the church, where his comrades have dragged him clear of the firing. The scuffles of youth have become actual war. "Both legs stuck out awkwardly. He had been hit in the spine." The day is hot. Rinaldi lies wounded face downward in the sun beside him. "You and me we've made a separate peace," says Nick, with conscious irony. "We're not patriots." Their peace, separating and painful, has been made not by them but for them, as Nick seems to realize. Philip Young has said that Hemingway's hero turns away, with a sweaty smile, from the society that has hurt him. Actually, Nick turns away from Rinaldi, who is too badly wounded to appreciate Nick's brave humor or the fact that the battle is going well, that they are out of it, that the stretchers are coming. Nick is grimly cheerful, badly hurt, but not shattered. Nevertheless, all the brutality recorded in *In Our Time* says that the world is wrong. Nick has tried to live with it but has had a separate tortured peace made for him—so this is peace in our time. Apparently, Nick's full shattering sense of separation is yet to come.

For "The Big Two-Hearted River" sums up the mental strain of such disillusion and such separation, as it sums up the book. Nick is absolutely alone. He has gone to Seney, in Michigan's upper peninsula, to fish and, as we gather more clearly from later stories, to keep his shell-shocked mind from disintegration. Everything in the story is tensely on the point of slippage, like the trout "keeping themselves steady in the current with wavering fins" —exactly Nick's state of mind, as Young has observed. Nick must deliberately keep from thinking, and Hemingway's tense unmeditative prose was never more expressively fitted to its subject. Again, like "The Battler," the story progresses from dark into light and then into dark again. Nick gets off the train to discover his destination completely burned out and black. He climbs out of the burned town into spacious country. He then fishes downstream toward the blackened town again and stops short of a dark and tangled swamp, where fishing would be "a tragic adventure."

Every sentence seems to sound a harmonic of larger and parallel meaning. And the key is the river, the stream of consciousness, of time, of life. Fishing, as later in *The Old Man and the Sea,* becomes a ritual symbolic of larger endeavor, as Cowley was first to observe in his "Introduction" to *The Portable Hemingway.* The story seems to bring together the hallucinatory effect of the preceding disjointed stories and sketches, as if all had been episodes in a dream of recollection and terror. The last sentence of the Maera sketch (*"Then he was dead"*) flows like a dream into the first sentence of "The Big Two-Hearted River": "The train went on up the track out of sight, around one of the hills of burnt timber." Between the two halves of the story is the hanging of a man too terrified to stand, while a priest, who doesn't have to do the dying, urges Hemingway's most central message on him: *"Be a man, my son"*—exactly what Nick is attempting to be on his lonely trip after the war. Again the sketch ends in death, as the trap falls; and again the story opens with a new awakening of consciousness as Nick crawls from his tent into the morning sun: "There was the meadow, the river and the swamp." Nick is, in fact, undergoing a kind of rebirth, as the reiterated birth and death throughout the book accumulates behind the story.

When Nick executes his trout by breaking their necks, reminding us of the hanged man of the preceding sketch, we can have little doubt that the swamp represents the darkness of death, of mental chaos, of unknowing and the unknown, the biggest mystery of life, and that to be a man Nick must face it, fishing again the blackened tangle of his wartime experience. "There were plenty of days coming when he could fish the swamp." The river has some big-hearted, two-hearted, black-hearted quality: the active stream and the dark swamp it leads to, the good and the evil, to be fished as an ultimate test of worth. The Big Two-Hearted River is life-and-death itself. The peace for which Nick is searching in our war-torn time is not unlike—in a tough earthbound way—that which passes all understanding.

Two stories in *Men Without Women* (1927) and one in *Winner Take Nothing* (1933) particularly clarify Nick's trip to the Two-Hearted. In "Now I Lay Me" a young American officer of Italian troops (whom we discover to be Nick) tells his story in the first person. When too near the front to keep a light burning, he fears that his soul will leave his body if he goes to sleep in the dark. He has been "blown up at night" in the early spring. He has been "wounded a couple of times" and was eventually to be hospitalized in Milan, wounded again in the coming October offensive. Hemingway, wounded in the summer, hospitalized in Milan, needing a nightlight for some time afterward, has blasted Nick's life in the spring and made life a succession of wounds until Nick, telling his story years later, speaks like a man in a daze.

Outside the window, silkworms are chewing and dropping on the leaves as steadily as Nick's own thoughts, helping to keep him awake in the dark. But his favorite method of keeping awake and keeping his soul in his body is to fish in his mind down "a trout stream I had fished along when I was a boy." It, too, has a swamp, a place of dire extremity where once he could "find no bait at all and had to cut up one of the trout I had caught and use him for bait." And sometimes he makes up streams as good as the ones he knows.

Some nights he cannot fish, so he says his prayers over and over, saying a Hail Mary and an Our Father for everyone he can remember as far back as he can go. Some nights he cannot even remember his prayers and "could only get as far as 'On earth as it is in heaven. . . .' " Later, he tries to remember all the girls he has known and to imagine how they would be as wives. His orderly, a naturalized Italian-American caught in the Italian army, with his wife running his restaurant for him in Chicago, thinks Nick should marry a nice Italian girl to solve all his problems. But Nick's imaginary girls blur; he goes back to fishing, and prays for his orderly, who, he adds years later as he tells the story, would probably be disappointed that he has never married. The orderly's fine comic characterization within the circle of Nick's anguish, the eccentric focus sharp beside the misery, as in "Out of Season," is Hemingway at his best, discovering the secret art of his novels. "Now I Lay Me" may be his best story, at least in the early, soft, "inner" mode.

"In Another Country" finishes Nick's marital lesson. Now it is fall. The young officer is undergoing physical therapy in a Milan hospital. Somewhat as in "Now I Lay Me," he keeps near the street lights and lies awake at night "afraid to die and wondering how I would be when I went back to the front again." The sad drifting voice is more lost than ever: "In the fall the war was always there, but we did not go to it any more. It was cold in the fall in Milan and the dark came very early." He is "in another country," alienated in every way, circle after circle: an American in Italy, an officer among people who shout "down with the officers," maimed among the healthy, separated from the war. But, most of all, he is alone even in his little group of wounded Italian officers because he knows that they had been brave and that his medals came only because he was American and wounded. He is an exile even among exiles, as in "The Battler."

But the story implies that none can escape, that all will be exiled, that nothing—not love nor marriage—will last. Hemingway has taken his title from the epigraph to T. S. Eliot's "Portrait of a Lady," itself a quotation from Marlowe's *Jew Of Malta*.[1] The young man's last alienation, it seems, is from sex and marriage and the continuity of settled life. He is fiercely advised not to marry, by a fellow cripple—another fine characterization, this time not far from center—a little Italian major who has just unexpectedly lost the young wife married only after his coming retirement had seemed to make marriage safe. The wench is dead, and in another country, and the whole story, as the narrator says, was "a long time ago." It ends with the major sitting lifelessly as the exercising machine slaps at the little withered hand that had once held the best rapier in Italy. This is Hemingway's world—although Robert Jordan and Colonel Cantwell and the Old Man, the undefeated losers, will begin to act in spite of it—a world crippling and alienating and indifferent, like a machine. The early Hemingway hero is a man acted upon until he is incapable of action, blasted into his deadened separate peace.

"A Way You'll Never Be" (1933) fills in some more and slightly inconsistent details of Nick's wartime experiences, and with a touch of scorn, as if Hemingway were beginning to tire of his hero. He is now "Nicholas" Adams, and is clearly unheroic, and closer to Hemingway the Red Cross soldier. He rides his bicycle down a

---

[1] Colonel Cantwell quotes it twenty-three years later, with another allusion to Eliot, in *Across the River and Into the Trees*. Here is Eliot's version as Hemingway would have known it, simply Marlowe's prose dialogue arranged as poetry:

> Thou has committed—
> Fornication: but that was in another country,
> And besides, the wench is dead.

Wide World Photos

ERNEST HEMINGWAY AT SUN VALLEY

sunken road to visit his former Italian battalion, sent in a concocted American uniform to advertise that the Yanks are coming. He "really has no rank." He says he should have brought chocolate and postcards.

Nick is recovering from a fractured skull and wounds "in various places"; he can't sleep without a light; he has previously been "certified as nutty"; his legs stiffen whenever they are out straight too long; he has attacks of jumbled memories and wild talk, but can control them somewhat. The town is Fossalta. Here are the mulberry leaves and the corpses amidst pillaged papers recorded in Hemingway's "Natural History of the Dead." Here are the sunken road, the canal, and the house across the river that Colonel Cantwell is to remember when he, like Nick, returns to the very spot where he (and Nick and Ernest Hemingway) was blown up thirty years before. Nick, haunted by dreams of Fossalta, is now back at the actual place:

He never dreamed about the front now any more but what frightened him so that he could not get rid of it was that long yellow house and the different width of the river. Now he was back here at the river, he had gone through the same town, and there was no house. Nor was the river that way. Then where did he go each night and what was the peril, and why would he wake, soaking wet, more frightened than he had ever been in a bombardment, because of a house and a long stable and a canal?

When Nick begins talking wildly about grasshoppers as fishing bait —"These insects at one time played a very important part in my life"—we see more clearly that Nick at the Two-Hearted River was visiting symbolic country.

When you stand on the track at Seney today, you can almost see the superimposition of Fossalta and the imaginary nocturnal rivers. The "sunken road" of Fossalta seems to have given Seney, actually as flat as a table top, a road with "a high, fire-scarred hill on either side," like the imaginary hill around which the train has disappeared, though the actual track lies as straight as a flat ladder to infinity—the longest straight track in Michigan. Furthermore, Hemingway has "burned out" Seney in the image of war-burned Fossalta: the sunken road, the burned town, then the river.

Of course, the image of Fossalta is only partially visible behind Hemingway's Seney. According to Robert Cantwell in *Sports Illustrated* (July 17, 1961), there was some kind of fire in Seney in 1919, the very year Nick would have visited it after the war (following Hemingway's own rustication to Walloon Lake on Michigan's lower peninsula, from which he may or may not have visited Seney on the upper one). But Seney has a more famous devastation by forest fire in its history, already in the glamorous past when Hemingway was born. It was burned out in the height of its lumberjacking glory in 1891, rebuilt, and partially burned out three or four years later. Moreover, at some time in Hemingway's boyhood the hotel (the White House, Hemingway's "Mansion House") burned down, as his poem "Along with Youth" shows—a poem written in the same burst of activity that produced the *in our time* sketches and the first work on "The Big Two-Hearted River." The dusty stuffed birds, the porcupine skin, the old letters and newspapers, all the contents of the boy's room are gone, "along with youth"—

> And the canoe that went to pieces on the beach
> The year of the big storm
> When the hotel burned down
> At Seney, Michigan.

36

In "The Big Two-Hearted River," in other words, Hemingway
moves Seney's famous burnings forward to "our time" to underwrite the symbolic effect of war-blackened towns with his full private
sense of a glorious, brawling past that is burned and lost, along
with youth.

Nick's spiritual climb in "The Big Two-Hearted River" has also
tilted flat Seney onto a hillside and made the flat road northward
climb a ridge of hills, as Nick drives his troubled forehead into
the tumpline of his load and climbs away from desolation and disappointment, and from the center of his wounding, the phantom
Fossalta. Hemingway has even made his brown grasshoppers turn
black, surviving on the charred land (a highly unlikely phenomenon,
according to some orthopterists). Nick, resting with legs straight
out, against a charred stump in exactly his position as he leans
against the church wall in the first sketch, examines a blackened
grasshopper and lets it go; the burning can be survived.

About "The Big Two-Hearted River" Hemingway wrote to Gertrude Stein (August 15, 1924) that he was "trying to do the country
like Cézanne," and that "the country is swell, I made it all up, so
I see it all and part of it comes out the way it ought to . . . ."
I made it all up. However one may wish to challenge this statement, one can see, standing at Seney, something of what Hemingway considered the creative process to be: a recapturing of
actuality in the visual memory and a touching of it with symbolic significance. His constant pursuit of "truth" leads to an uncomfortably
high factual component in his fiction—and to an uncomfortably high
fictional component in his factual statements about himself—all fact
so becoming fiction in his view that he no longer wishes to distinguish
the two.

His work, up through the alchemy of *A Farewell to Arms,* is really
quintessential journalism, dreamed into fiction. And the power in
Hemingway's journalistic art lies in its intensely suggested meaning
—which depends on never being stated, always being poised, like
a trout, under the noncommittal surface. His bell-like prose makes
resonant the slightest poetic suggestion: former happiness on the
shore of the Black River, fishing the Big Two-Hearted River toward
the final swamp.

The Black River is a real Michigan river (there are two of
them), and so is the Two Hearted (no hyphen) with branches referred
to as Big and Little. But the Two Hearted does not run through
Seney. It lies some forty rugged miles to the northeast—too far
for Nick to have hiked in an afternoon that included a nap even

if he had gone in the right direction. The river which runs through Seney, which Nick contemplates from the bridge, on which he camps upstream to the northwest, is the Fox. Hemingway has simply borrowed a more symbolic, though actual, name.

It is as if Lieutenant Nick of "Now I Lay Me," not Hemingway, had written "The Big Two-Hearted River" from one of his imaginary streams that, as Lieutenant Nick says, "are confused with streams I really know. I gave them all names and went to them on the train and sometimes walked for miles to get to them." The Fox River at Seney, the stream both reached by train and walked to for miles, the stream Hemingway "really knew," seems to be Lieutenant Nick's perpetual model; and Hemingway too has given it a name (borrowed) and confused it with imagination. Lieutenant Nick goes back down the stream of time, as it were, to remember things as far back toward birth as he can. He remembers when his mother burned his father's boyhood relics (the best ones "went all to pieces") and his father raked what he could from the blackened ruins. Seney, too, is a burnt relic of boyhood, and Fossalta one of youth, as if author Nick had taken a river in his head he had fished in the dark to keep his sanity and had sent hero Nick along it on the same mission, fishing a real river as symbolic antidote to insanity and the terror of violent pain and violent death.

Beyond Seney's imaginary symbolic hills, the country Nick traverses along the Fox is almost exactly as Hemingway describes it, with a swift, deep, clear-brown river bridged by fallen logs, and a suitable swamp or two, though none directly in the river's path. Hemingway has given the place his magic, as he sent his mind back from another country in 1923 to recapture and "make up" a trip he made, or imagined he made, in 1919.

৽৽ ৡ৵

When Hemingway wrote "The Big Two-Hearted River," following the sketches of Nick wounded and of the bombardment at Fossalta, he was just beginning to probe his wounds. He certainly did not know all the details of Nick's biography-to-come, nor could he have seen the full depth of his meaning. He knew, certainly, that he was getting more than surface: he urged doubting friends to re-read the story; he later declared in *Green Hills of Africa* that, with dedication and luck, prose can be carried to a fourth and fifth dimension. But it is characteristic of Hemingway's incantation to keep his eye steadily on the object without looking at the spirits invoked, pretending even to himself that they are not there. This objective magic is strongest in "The Big Two-Hearted River" and in its two best commentaries, "In Another Country" and "Now I Lay Me," because the mind of the hero exactly suits the incantation. Nick, too, is keeping his eye straight ahead for fear of the ghosts, and all the wells of resentment and sweet self-pity flow tightly under the surface of the swift brown prose. Hemingway's descant over the losses of youth is never better.

"Fathers and Sons," Hemingway's last story about Nick—last in his last book of stories—presents Nick, now thirty-eight, a traveling salesman, with a son of his own. Hemingway is "studying the death of his father," as he was to say later in *Death in the After-noon*: ". . . I had never been able to study [violent] deaths as a man might, for instance, study the death of his father or the hanging of some one . . . ." He begins with a faint note of scorn for his former self: here, too, Nick is "Nicholas" Adams. But soon it is Nick again; and the story is a moving meditation on the virtual impossibility of good fatherhood. Nick is grateful for his father's teaching him to hunt; he knows that his father was poor on sex. He remembers how he "loved his father but hated the smell of him." The Indian girl, Trudy, comes again to mind. His son wakes up in the car beside him and asks about the Indians. Nick of course can no more tell his son what he knows of sex than could his father whom the grandson reveres because he, too, lived with the Indians. The story is a tribute to Hemingway's father, resented and loved:

> The big frame, the quick movements, the wide shoulders, the hooked, hawk nose, the beard that covered the weak chin, you never thought about—it was always the eyes. They were protected in his head by the formation of the brows; set deep as though a special protection had been devised for some very valuable instrument.

Dr. Hemingway's penetrating black eyes still look out from the photographs, as memorable as Nick says they are, and as Young has already noted. And though Hemingway had apparently used up all he had to say about himself as Nick Adams, he continued to study his father's death, and he progressively took on his father's image with all its fears—first the hunter and fisher, then the bearded Papa, then the final gun.

39

3

✑ JAKE BARNES AND SPRING TORRENTS

NICK ADAMS was soon to become Jake Barnes, as Hemingway mixed Paris into his war and alienation. He had continued to work daily, the most serious writer anyone seems to have known, a shy, cheerful, vigorous young man in sneakers and a jacket with one leathered elbow. He had an agreeable wife and "an infant son named Bumby who had been trained to put up his fists and assume a ferocious expression," one apparently "not as ferocious as his father would have liked," according to Harold Loeb's *The Way It Was*.

Loeb is the Robert Cohn of *The Sun Also Rises,* the first draft of which Hemingway wrote in a driving month and a half, directly after his friendship with Loeb exploded at the fiesta in Pamplona in July, 1925. Hemingway said that he had written "too fast each day to the point of complete exhaustion." After another three weeks he tossed off *The Torrents of Spring* in a little more than a week in November—after he "had finished the first draft of *The Sun Also Rises*, to cool out."

The Torrents of Spring, like the more important book that caused it, is an attack on former friends. It is chiefly a parody of Sherwood Anderson's *Dark Laughter*. Hemingway's first section is "Red and Black Laughter," and a Negro's laugh echoes an Indian war whoop at chapter endings. The title is from a novel by Turgenev, whose *Sportsman's Sketches* Anderson admired as "the sweetest thing in all literature," a book Jake Barnes had read more than once, and one Hemingway later honored in the *Green Hills of Africa* and in lists of recommended reading. Turgenev's *Torrents of Spring* tells of love forsaken in springtime lust; and Hemingway remakes Anderson's internal stirrings into a springtime thaw at a Petoskey pump factory, leading Scripps O'Neil from one waitress to another and then "out into the night, out into the night" (and the snow) after a naked squaw. Occasionally the book is funny, and the parody good: "Where had he been? Had he been in an Indian club? What was it all about? Was this the end?" This does sound like Anderson's interior tremolo; and making a surreptitious clubroom for Indians into a momentary wooden "Indian club" lifts imitation into hilarity. Even better is a passage about hero O'Neil, who has just sold a story to George Horace Lorimer (in actuality, editor of *The Saturday Evening Post,* whose name coincided happily with that of Hemingway's own editor, Horace Liveright):

> Scripps striding through the Lake Country with Wordsworth. A field of golden daffodils. The wind blowing at Windermere. Far off, perhaps, a stag at bay. Ah, that was farther north, in Scotland. They were a hardy race, those Scots, deep in their mountain fastnesses. Harry Lauder and his pipe.

And more. There are moments of real hilarity concocted from the literarily worn and false.

But the mixture is more often tasteless. Gertrude Stein comes in for her helping. H. L. Mencken is coupled in the dedication with S. Stanwood Menken, a true-blue American with whom confusion was infuriating—but the jest smacks of expediency rather than conviction. Hemingway indeed lacks conviction and indignation sufficient to sustain his highjinks. He quotes Fielding on the Ridiculous, and either misses Fielding's point (that actuality furishes ample comedy) or cannot illustrate it—or thinks the statement itself is fusty and antique. He attempts a Fieldingesque repartee with the reader, a poor thing not his own that is also to muddle *Death in the Afternoon.* Though he could catch beautifully the painful comedy of Nick's boyhood, though he could banter nicely in private, as his letters show, though he could write unequaled dialogue that jests at scars and could sketch to perfection the comic personality just off center-stage, he found the main show deadly serious; and his Ridiculous becomes ridiculous.

Consequently, the self-parody frequently charged against Hemingway's weaker moments is sadly apparent in *The Torrents of Spring.* Hemingway intends some of it, as in that hybrid of newspaper and creativity, Scripps O'Neil: Hemingway mocking himself as a combination of the Scripps-Howard press and Eugene O'Neill. And again, "Windermere" was the name of the Hemingways' summer home at Walloon Lake, a name chosen by Mrs. Hemingway from her admired Sir Walter Scott. This fun is intentional. But Hemingway's self-parody is also unintentional. The story is set in Nick Adams's Michigan heartland, with coincidences of self-mockery beyond anything Hemingway could have seen clearly. Nick, too,

41

loved a local waitress. Here again are the Indians (now actually speaking of the White Father and Manitou) and the Peerless tobacco and the railroad tracks of Hemingway's high-school story. Here is the wounded veteran inhibited from sexual intercourse and troubled—a cooling out of Jake Barnes indeed. He is another Krebs, who wants to talk about the war and cannot convey the truth of it: two Indian veterans, who do not need to talk about it, doubt that Yogi Johnson was even in it. And Hemingway, no longer comic, seems to bloody the facts as much as "that fellow Anderson" had made them pallid: "Most of the men he had known had been excited as hell when they had first killed. The trouble was to keep them from killing too much." With Yogi Johnson we are momentarily in Hemingway's private hell, where the truth always comes out the color of fiction, and the fiction always colors the truth.

And here is the Hemingway prose, which he cannot help writing as he parodies styles too near his own: "There were a pile of deer shipped down by hunters from the Upper Peninsula of Michigan, lying piled the one on the other, dead and stiff and drifted half over with snow on the station platform." Omit the slight parodic inflation (beginning with "shipped" and running through "the one on the other"), and we are indeed "In Another Country"—to be written sometime after March the next year: "There was much game hanging outside the shops, and the snow powdered in the fur of the foxes and the wind blew their tails. The deer hung stiff and heavy and empty, and small birds blew in the wind and the wind turned their feathers." Hemingway cannot keep from writing like himself. The Indian clubroom has real moments; the drummer in the beanery is Hemingway at his incidental best. But the book itself is an embarrassment.

The *Torrents* cooled Hemingway off, at the expense of former friends, and at his own expense: hysteria vaguely lurks behind the hilarity, as it was later effectively to do in Nick's mad talk of grasshoppers, in "A Way You'll Never Be." Somewhere uneasily in the background is Hemingway's narcissistic obsession, Hemingway vaguely picking at himself in the dark, Hemingway attacking as untrue the art he is making out of his own shadows, and punishing himself for distorting into fiction the personal truth he cannot locate, a faint foreshadowing of the final untrue self-disgust that led to suicide.

The Sun Also Rises had also begun as an attack on a former friend and also represents a considerable measure of self-punishment. Hemingway had met Harold Loeb in the fall of 1923 at one of Ford Madox Ford's weekly teas, and Loeb had then sought out his friendship. His mother was a Guggenheim; his father, of the family famous for the Loeb Classical Library. Harold Loeb was now the rich young angel of a New York little magazine, and had a novel nearly finished. Soon he and Hemingway were playing tennis, boxing between sets, dining together, playing bridge, talking about writing.

In August, 1924, Liveright accepted Loeb's *Doodab*. In September, Hemingway and Loeb "made plans for skiing that winter in Austria, trout fishing in the spring on a very special Spanish river, and then going on to the bullfights in Pamplona." In October, Hemingway and Loeb went to Senlis, where, over a long, murderous two-man poker game in the hotel room, Hemingway's antagonism momentarily broke out.

Very soon, after a dozen oysters and two bottles of wine, Loeb, the successful novelist, presumed to advise his friend about writing. Hemingway needed to put in some women, Loeb said, suggesting that Hemingway's happy marriage had robbed him of necessary misery. Again Hemingway flared, and then told of his lost "English" nurse in Milan. Next, Loeb took Hemingway to meet Leon Fleischman, with whom Loeb had just signed his Liveright contract. Hemingway disliked him at once but sent him the *In Our Time* manuscript. In December, the Hemingways and party went skiing in Austria, Loeb promising to follow after settling the editorial affairs of *Doodab*.

From Austria, Hemingway wrote Loeb wishing he were there and asking him to get his book back from Fleischman: he had learned that Donald Ogden Stewart had sent another version of it to the Doran company. But the book had already gone to New York. Loeb decided to sail for New York himself to settle his own editorial questions and perhaps to help out good old Hem. And indeed he did. He dropped into Liveright's just in time to persuade the manuscript reader to give *In Our Time* another reading. When it was accepted by Liveright, Loeb cabled Hemingway in Austria. On February 27, 1925, Hemingway got Loeb's cable and a similar one from Stewart (now also interceding with Liveright). Hemingway immediately wrote Loeb his thanks and many questions, particularly asking if his book would make fall publication along with Loeb's. He returned to Paris elated, only to be piqued again when

43

Loeb told him of the rescue. Anderson too had claimed an assist, as did Stewart, and now Loeb. It looked as if he needed help from half of New York.

In the spring, Bill Smith, Hemingway's boyhood summer friend in Michigan, arrived. He and Loeb became friends, matching Hemingway and Paul Fisher at tennis, dining together when Hemingway, the married man, had to leave for home. The Hemingways had already met Lady Duff Twysden (Loeb makes it "Twitchell"), a tweedy British Circe, and her lover, Pat Guthrie (Loeb's "Swazey"). It was Paris in the spring. Spain and fishing and Pamplona were just ahead. And the cast of *The Sun Also Rises* had gathered.

Then in June, Harold Loeb slipped off to St.-Jean-de-Luz with Duff Twysden. The rich young Jew, the Princeton man, Coach Spider Kelly's shining bantam with the handsomely flattened nose, who could outplay Hemingway at tennis and outbox his twitching eye, who had beaten him to publication and then had too fortunately helped him—had run off with the most desirable woman in Paris. Hemingway was certainly jealous, and certainly in love with her, though Duff's friendly respect for Hadley seems to have kept him at a pleasantly miserable distance.

Loeb stayed on at St.-Jean-de-Luz after Duff went back to Pat Guthrie, just back from a mission to London and mother for money. Hemingway asked them to come along on the fishing and bullfighting party. Duff and Pat decided to stay in St.-Jean-de-Luz until time for the fights. Loeb, hoping for another chance, wired that he too would skip the fishing and would meet Hemingway in Pamplona on Monday, July 6, 1925.

The St.-Jean-de-Luz threesome was far from happy. Guthrie was jealous; Duff had arrived wearing not her usual slouched hat but a beret on the Hemingway pattern; and Loeb was uneasy about his *coup de boudoir* and the evident complications with Hemingway. The three drove to Pamplona on Sunday, July 5.

For Hemingway, Hadley, Bill Smith, and Donald Stewart, the fishing had gone sour. Hemingway's editor had delayed their start (June 24 or 25); a new reservoir had spoiled their stream. They had caught nothing. They arrived in Pamplona on Monday, July 6, 1925. But spirits revived after drinks and lunch. Everyone went to watch the bulls unloaded, and the fiesta was on.

Tuesday morning, Hemingway, Smith, and Loeb tried the crowded amateur cowfighting (with the Amazonian cows of the fighting breed, as it would seem from Loeb's pictures and Hemingway's explana-

tion in *Death in the Afternoon.*) Then came a day of fights, with
Hemingway enthusiastic about Cayetano Ordonez, Niño de la Palma.
Next morning Hemingway, Smith, and Loeb again tried the amateur
run. Loeb, turning to save himself, rode across the arena seated
between the cow's horns, to be tossed in the air and to land on his
feet. Smith made one good pass with his jacket and received one
butting. Hemingway grabbed a cow's horns from behind and bull-
dogged her to the ground to the crowd's delight. New York pho-
tographers caught Loeb and Smith in action, but missed Hemingway, except once as background. Hemingway had already met
Niño de la Palma, who spoke with amused admiration of Loeb's (not
Hemingway's) bullfighting. Loeb seemed to be upstaging him at
every turn.

   Thursday, July 9, brought the explosion. On Wednesday after
dinner, Hadley had gone to her room with a headache, and Hemingway with her. Guthrie wandered off. Loeb and Duff Twysden
went off for a quiet drink, which led to someone's party and eventually to Loeb dead drunk and Duff off on the town. She came to
lunch on Thursday with a black eye and a bruised forehead. For
the afternoon fights, Duff and Guthrie moved up to sit with the
Hemingways, and Smith and Stewart moved down with Loeb. Dinner was silent and strained. Then Hemingway began to needle
Loeb about his coolness toward bullfighting. Guthrie joined in.
Until finally:

   "Look here," said Pat. "I may be dumb. I may be useless. But
I know enough to stay away when I'm not wanted."
   "Is that how you got through school?" [asked Loeb.]
   "You lay off Pat," said Hem grimly. "You've done enough to
spoil this party."

They told Loeb to get out. Loeb said he would "the instant Duff
wants it." Duff said she did not want it. "You lousy bastard,"
said Hemingway. "Running to a woman." Loeb then invited Hemingway out. They walked solemnly toward a dark corner. Loeb
was afraid, he remembers, because he knew he could not outbox a
big and angry Hemingway. He also knew their friendship was over:

   I was tremendously sad—so sad that for a moment I forgot to be
afraid. It was my pattern, I felt, slowly, gradually, to acquire a
friend and then have him turn in an instant into a bitter, lashing
enemy. It had happened at Princeton and Mohegan, and in The Sun-
wise Turn [his bookshop]. Even in marriage. There was something
about me. I felt excruciatingly lonely . . . .

Loeb put his glasses in his jacket and looked for a safe place to hang it. "Shall I hold it for you?" grinned Hemingway, and the battle was off.

Everyone pretended that nothing had happened. Hemingway put a heartfelt apology in Loeb's box. They stayed through the fiesta (from July 7 to 11, by Hemingway's calendar in *Death in the Afternoon*). On the last day Niño de la Palma earned the bull's ear and presented it to Hadley; and he and the Hemingways left for Madrid. In *Death in the Afternoon* (1932), Hemingway remembers:

> Hadley, with the bull's ear wrapped in a handkerchief, the ear was very stiff and dry and the hair all wore off it and the man who cut the ear is bald now too and slicks long strips of hair over the top of his head and he was a beau then. He was, all right.

Duff, Guthrie, Smith, and Loeb drove back to St.-Jean-de-Luz together.

Ten days later in Valencia, on July 21, 1925, his twenty-sixth birthday, Hemingway started *The Sun Also Rises*. He wrote through the rest of July and all of August, in Valencia, Madrid, St. Sebastian, and Hendaye, following the fights, and vacationing where Jake Barnes is to vacation. He finished the first draft in Paris on September 6, 1925. He relaxed for the rest of September, then turned to *The Torrents of Spring*. He went to ski in Austria for the rest of November and December. He started rewriting *The Sun Also Rises* in January, 1926, and took a trip to New York in February. By the end of March he had finished, cutting almost a third (40,-000 words) of his first draft. Scribner's published it on October 22, 1926.

The Sun Also Rises starts as a satirical portrait of Robert Cohn, who sees the world as W. H. Hudson's *Purple Land* and the abandoned Brett as "absolutely fine and straight." The portrait is penetrating, sympathetic, and scandalously close to the details of Loeb's life, exactly catching the plaintive romantic whom Loeb reveals in his own book, the pathetic good guy with "a nice, boyish sort of cheerfulness that had never been trained out of him." Loeb actually speaks of Hudson's South America, and thinks of the fallen woman as an angel with the voice of a bird. Loeb confesses his gift for irritating people with his need for friendship and recognition, and with his non-Hemingway incidence of good luck. On his high escapade with Duff Twysden, he drew a perfect bridge hand. "You *would* get thirteen hearts," she said. She told him that she was not sure he belonged to her "esoteric circle." Discussing the Hemingways, she said that perhaps Loeb was "not one of us after all."

This is indeed Cohn of *The Sun Also Rises*, the outsider so earnestly wanting in. Brett repeatedly tells Jake that Count Mippipopolous is "one of us"; and it is clear that Cohn is not. He is not an *aficionado*. *Afición*, the freemasonry of bullfighting, can excuse almost any defect. Montoya, the hotelkeeper, immediately forgives Barnes his tourist friends: "Without his ever saying anything they were simply a little something shameful between us, like the spilling open of the horses in bullfighting." So it is with the defects within the Paris group—Brett's infidelities, Mike's weaknesses, Harvey Stone's drink—a little shameful but within the esoteric circle of the lost, a circle that inexorably excludes Cohn, the unrealist still living by Victorian mottoes, springing to arms over imaginary insults to a nonexistent lady, trying to be well lost but never making it.

By the beginning of the third chapter, Jake Barnes's attention has shifted from Robert Cohn to himself:

> It was a warm spring night and I sat at a table on the terrace of the Napolitain after Robert had gone, watching it get dark and the electric signs come on, and the red and green stop-and-go traffic-signal, and the crowd going by, and the horse-cabs clippety-clopping along at the edge of the solid taxi traffic, and the *poules* going by, singly and in pairs, looking for the evening meal.

The slow attractive dirge on being lost and doomed has begun. Barnes picks up a sour little prostitute "because of a vague sentimental idea that it would be nice to eat with some one," excusing himself from sexual intercourse on the grounds that he is "sick." "Everybody's sick," says the girl. Jake's peculiar wistfulness, a poetic hyperbole of everybody's sickness, is soon explained: the war has left him a sexual cripple, incapable of ever escaping from loneliness into consummated love.

"You are all a lost generation," said Gertrude Stein to Hemingway; and he took her sentence as his epigraph, together with an old echo from Ecclesiastes—which, he stated much later, was intended as a refutation of lostness: "One generation passeth away, and another generation cometh; but the earth abideth forever. . . . The sun also ariseth, and the sun goeth down, and hasteth to the place where he arose. . . ." But to say that the sun *also* rises is to emphasize that it has set. The sun also rises, yes, and the earth abides, yes; but our generation is no longer here to rise nor to stay; and the ancient classical sadness of this fact echoes Biblically and beautifully underneath everything in Barnes's meditation on the past, underneath the bright moments, the happiness of getting away from it all with a sound friend, the pleasures of countryside and fiesta and bullfight.

Jake Barnes represents the best of the lost generation, the best that is lost. Barnes is the maimed knight of the lost. As Mark Spilka suggests, in his "The Death of Love in *The Sun Also Rises*," Barnes is uncomfortably similar to Cohn, the romantic knight in full flower; and he is sadly incapable of the self-sufficient manhood of Romero, the bullfighter, who has drawn the sportsman's independent contest to a point of steely beauty in spite of the wasted world. Jake is powerless between the two, in spite of a decent stoicism in a lost world, with a decent community of lost spirit and a measure of existential courage for getting on with a bad job.

His crowd is not only a generation lost: it has lost its powers of generation in turn. It is lost from the succession of generations on which the sun will rise and set and rise again. Barnes is a newspaperman, an ex-avaitor made impotent by war, wounded in a way usually considered comic while "flying on a joke front like the Italian." Sent to recuperate in England, he has met Lady Brett Ashley, a member of the Voluntary Aid Detachment of amateur nurses and helpers. They have fallen in love and tried some sort of consummation: "I don't want to go through that hell again," says Brett, who still cannot keep from seeing him. Jake's wound has wounded her too, and helped to turn her into the siren of Paris and Pamplona.

Now it is Paris, 1924.[1] Jake is living alone, working hard, treating himself and the world with decent irony and pity—as Bill Gorton is to recommend ironically—except that it "is awfully easy to be hard-boiled about everything in the daytime, but at night it is another thing." He looks at his maimed self in the mirror, placed *à la mode* beside the bed. He turns out the light. His head "starts to work." Once, for six months he had "never slept with the electric light off."

[1] Dated by Romero's age and birth year, and oddly authenticated by mention of Charles Ledoux—Ch. IX—who forfeited his European featherweight title on June 25, 1924, by refusing a challenge; for this nonexistent fight, Hemingway supplies a fictional opponent, apparently a version of the "Ad Francis" in "The Battler." Hemingway has apparently placed his story a year earlier than the actual events as part of the fictional disguise.

Jake is, of course, another Lieutenant Nick, who lays him down but cannot sleep, the crippled hero able to pray only in a hopeless way, a Catholic knowing that the Church is right in its advice to forget one's self, but knowing that it is impossible to do so, hoping that someday he will be a better Catholic but knowing that there is really no hope. Like Nick, Jake is one whom the civilized world and its wars have cut away from their generations, the essential motherless child of conflagration, the young man without woman ("To hell with women, anyway. To hell with you, Brett Ashley").

Hemingway's persistent exclusion of his own marriage from the adolescent heartland of rod and gun and mountain air emphasizes the callow yearning of his masculine ideality. While actually skiing with his wife and others, he writes of two young men skiing alone against the shadow of a pregnant wife somewhere else. Following an unsuccessful fishing trip with his wife and others, he writes a masculine idyl of wood and stream. Following a fiesta with his wife, and a trip to Madrid with his wife and the bullfighter they had befriended, he writes an idyl about the Belle Dame sans Merci and a male beautifully and sadly inside the magic circle because impotent and now forever invulnerable, and forever lost.

The energy in the book comes directly from this magic spring. Hemingway, working so close to the facts of Loeb, Twysden, and Pamplona as almost to seem mere journalist, has touched a primal pulsation of mythology: the unearthly and unquenchable mythic appeal of the sorceress who, in spite of herself and with a regretful sigh, must emasculate the men she attracts. The romantic Cohn calls Brett Ashley a Circe who "turns men into swine," an idea scorned as literary by the inner circle of realists; but Hemingway plays along with the British expression "swine" through several succeeding pages, and Brett becomes the goddess of the wild fiesta that wrecks all their relationships except that of the two impotent lovers, the sorceress and her victim. Jake sees Brett through the crowd "walking, her head up, as though the fiesta were being staged in her honor, and she found it pleasant and amusing." Earlier, some dancers in wreaths of garlic have put her inside their circle: "They wanted her as an image to dance around"; after the dance they rush her to a wineshop and enthrone her on a cask. The friends pick up the humor and "translate" her to the hotel like a holy image.

Hemingway may simply be reporting; he certainly is not attempting any elaborate mythical parallel. But the mythical tracings are there, and extend through the whole book. Mike has "behaved badly" and, in Brett's words, has been "a swine." Jake says that everyone behaves badly with the proper chance. "You wouldn't behave badly," says Brett. And Jake is indeed ultimately decent, the crippled Catholic among pagans: he first slips into swinedom in the baiting of Cohn and is disgusted with his satisfaction in it. Jake remains the paragon of the lost. Bill Gorton, who at first seems a steady center, able, sympathetic, but above the battle, slips into swine-calling companionship with Mike (against previous victims of Mike's sponging), only to have Mike sponge on him at last: "Bill's face sort of changed." In the end, it is the emasculate Jake who rescues the lady in distress, as he and she silently knew he would—Jake, wiser and sadder because he knows he can behave badly and can betray the fellowship of bullfighting by pandering for his siren, a steer leading the bull to the slaughter.

For Circe must emasculate her lovers: unman them into caricatures of the lust that took their manhood, swine forever beneath her favors. Brett is not all Circe, of course; Hemingway simply works out the paradigm of siren and emasculation from his own private preoccupations. But like Circe, Brett must have an ever new man to replace the ones she drains.

Looking lovely, she sees the palm of Romero's bullfighting hand potent of "thousands of bulls." She has previously responded to a bull's power, looking down at "the great hump of muscle on his neck swollen tight": "My God, isn't he beautiful?" Jake and his friends are uncomfortably aware that Jake is a steer, making accidental references as they try to overlook it. Emasculation dins sadly through the book from Jake's whim with the prostitute onward. "Must be swell being a steer," says Bill, as Jake explains the herding of bulls by docile steers doomed to be hurt—exactly Jake's eventual function, herding the bullfighter in for Brett. "Why do you follow Brett around like a poor bloody steer?" Mike shouts at Cohn; and, as Spilka has noted, we are reminded that this is what Jake too, in painful literalness, is also doing. "Tell him bulls have no balls," shouts drunken Mike at the bullfighter, trying to drive him away from Brett. And when Don Manuel Orquito attempts to launch his fire balloons, we have a pathetic symbol of the whole fiesta from Jake's emasculate point of view: "The people shouted as each new luminous paper bubble careened, caught fire, and fell." "Globos illuminados," Mike said. "A bunch of bloody globos illuminados."

Testicles and the lack of testicles—an idea Hemingway consistently associates with bullfighting, using the Spanish slang *cojones*

—are clearly symbols of power and failure in *The Sun Also Rises*. Nevertheless, Hemingway was to say in his interview with George Plimpton thirty years later:

> Who ever said Jake was "emasculated precisely as is a steer"? Actually he had been wounded in quite a different way and his testicles were intact and not damaged. Thus he was capable of all normal feelings as a *man* but incapable of consummating them. The important distinction is that his wound was physical and not psychological and that he was not emasculated.

But whatever Hemingway's private picture of Jake's disfigurement and however that picture may have changed over the years, the similarity of Jake's deprivation to that of a steer is too insistent to be set aside. To be sure, Hemingway's later description of Jake as a man with no penis uncovers a horror in the Hemingway imagination of which there is much veiled evidence in his work and in anecdotes of his own lacks and sensitivities.[1] This picture of Jake would fit the evidence of the book, with the references to steers simply touching a general symbology too close for comfort. Jake remains a man, as Hemingway says, with normal feelings but with crippled capability, living with perpetual frustration.

The story of Jake Barnes is really one of education: "Perhaps as you went along you did learn something. I did not care what it was all about. All I wanted to know was how to live in it." How to live in a shattered world is Jake's problem, and he is educated to the reality of just how lost his generative island with its Circe really is, awakening finally on the cold hillside. Jake is educated to its ruin, and to his own, as he slowly changes from the man who keeps asking Brett if they can't "do something about it" to the man who can say to Brett's final wish as to how nice it might have been between them: "Yes, . . . Isn't it pretty to think so?" Spilka has well pointed out the nature of Barnes's education, his final realization that, even without his wound, he and Brett would be cases of arrested development, canceled out of the scheme of generation in a world where love and religion seem defunct, the two of them put in their places by Romero, who is living cleanly and manfully in a dangerous world and paying the bill. It never could have been nice between Jake and Brett. Jake has finally seen the distinction between this lost world as it is, in which one can have none of the dreams, and that romantic world where lovers live happily ever

---

[1] See Hemingway's fury at Max Eastman's apparent reference to inches in Loeb, *The Way It Was* (p. 252).

after. He has seen himself betray Romero into the siren's arms, and felt the scorn of Montoya; he knows that there is nothing left but to play the impotent knight to his fatal lady, the helplessly deceitful steer.

Brett, too, is educated to the truth of lost generation. She has found her match in the virile killer of bulls, the "lovely boy" fifteen years her junior. He breaks her, in effect, in her only fragility: "Brett was radiant . . . . 'I feel altogether changed . . . . '" The bullfighter has almost changed the siren into a woman, breaking her with self-realization at last. She refuses him, of course: "I'm thirty-four, you know. I'm not going to be one of those bitches that ruins children." She is too old, already out of the scheme of generation. She realizes, indirectly, that she, who has seemed a super-woman, is not even completely a woman at all. The bullfighter has thought her not womanly enough. Her hair is short and boyish. She remains a personification (as indeed she seems almost to have been in real life) of sex without responsibility, the male dream fulfilled, the everlasting initial female, the siren. She realizes that she too is impotent, one of the lost: "I can't even marry Mike," she says, in her moment of truth. And the book ends with the two impotent lovers, just touching as the taxi jounces, thinking how nice it might have been—or at least how pretty to think so.

As both Spilka and Carlos Baker (in his *Hemingway, the Writer as Artist*) have noticed in different ways, *The Sun Also Rises* is a species of chivalric romance after all, in its very demolition of the romantic dream. As Spilka says, Hemingway's protagonists "are deliberately shaped as allegorical figures"; and one measure of that shaping is Hemingway's giving Brett the illusion, apparently not in her actual counterpart's mind, that she and Mike would someday marry. One dream falls, but a still sweeter romantic agony remains. "It might have been"—no sweeter words of tongue or pen—continues to shimmer over the ruins left by "never could have been." This is the force behind the siren's cry. As the troubadours knew, the real sweetness of love is its unfulfillment. Hemingway has written the courtly romance for moderns, tough, dissonant, yet echoing forever the ancient sweetness of being forever lovelorn and forever longing, all underlined by the final knowledge of damnation, knowing that it never could have been, yet doomed to think that it might.

Hemingway's persistent yet buried self-pity has at last turned to the great romantic subject of love. He has amusingly come around to the very advice with which Harold Loeb had so infuriated him—

to put women into his writing—including not only Loeb's own Lady Duff, but also something of the nurse, of whom he then told Loeb, who threw him into the agony of hopeless longing, the central romantic passion and the buried center of *The Sun Also Rises,* the nurse about whom he had already written "A Very Short Story" and would soon write *A Farewell to Arms.*

"It might have been" echoes sweetly and painfully beneath everything Jake Barnes thinks and does, made resonant by his admirably tough and stoic surface, even after we close the book on his final acceptance of his emotional and moral impotence. How nice it might have been to have picked up a companionable girl, and dined and drunk and bedded. How nice to have found comfort in the Church. How nice to have been with Brett from start to finish, to have done what Cohn had done. How nice, in the beautiful fishing interlude, if one could really get away, and get away from women, and make it last, and fish with Bill and the lonely Harris again. How nice to be a boy with a girl on a raft. And, yes, at the end, how nice to be safely lost and a good consort to the lost —two together in a bar, with a polite and efficient bartender, and the perfect martini and the olive.

There it is, and there it will always be: the troubadour of the roaring twenties catching the beautiful and the damned, with irony and pity, in the delicious chill of the iced glass, the quiet moment for two, aware of the sweet sad glow before the fraying of the dream. He has really outdone his friend Fitzgerald. *The Sun Also Rises* is a wonderful book because it hits so deadly center the pathetic and unadmirable wish that will not die, the pleasure in wishful unfulfillment, the pleasure in pitying ourselves for not getting what we think we deserve. And the pity carries over into what Vergil called "the tears of things," as Hemingway's stream of sensuousness (in *Time* magazine's phrase) carries us along, the bell-like Biblical and classical sadness in the fact that for us the things of this world must pass, even though the sun can rise again. The sad wonder of life flows before us, caught as it was at the moment, never to return but always to be.

Things stay in the reader's mind: the girl looking absently away from her boxing puppets, "the sad tables of the Rotonde," the Basque cutting off a stream of wine with his teeth, the spat of rope-soled shoes dancing, the craftsman jumping on his wineskins to prove them sound, barges on the river, mountains with aged beech trees and "smooth grass, very green and fresh." Yet, strangely, Hemingway is not a sensuous writer. There is no metaphorical packing and no reticulated detail to help us see and feel distinctly. All is understated; all is bare outline. The reader is surprised at how much he himself is importing to fill it out. Hemingway picks the detail that calls forth the nod:

> After a while we came out of the mountains, and there were trees along both sides of the road, and a stream and ripe fields of grain, and the road went on, very white and straight ahead, and then lifted to a little rise, and off on the left was a hill with an old castle, with buildings close around it and a field of grain going right up to the walls and shifting in the wind. I was up in front with the driver and I turned around. Robert Cohn was asleep, but Bill looked and nodded his head.

The general outlines, which Carlos Baker has likened to those of the eighteenth century, ask from us the understanding nod we are flattered to be asked to give: simply "an old castle," which we immediately complete with whatever we need and know. The general idea and the bare hint suffices our worldly knowledge, in secret collusion with the author.

The clipped essentiality of the dialogue, frequently and justly admired, operates in much the same way. The characters themselves are understaters, and we get their understatement further selected for sharp illustration, the detail of idiom caught alive, full of momentary quip and amusement, and full of instant revelations of character:

> "Are you a sadist, Brett?" I asked.
> "Hope not."
> "He said Brett was a sadist just because she has a good. healthy stomach."
> "Won't be healthy long."

Or Mike, wishing Cohn were in jail for knocking him down:

> "Oh, no," said Edna. "You don't mean that."
> "I do, though," Mike said. "I'm not one of these chaps likes being knocked about. I never play games, even."
> Mike took a drink.
> "I never liked to hunt, you know. There was always the danger of having a horse fall on you. . . ."

Even the superb, hurt chatter of Frances is finally reduced to suggestion only, as Jake can stand no more and looks back through a window:

Frances was talking on to him, smiling brightly, looking into his face each time she asked: "Isn't it so, Robert?" Or maybe she did not ask that now. Perhaps she said something else.

The truth for which Hemingway strove is perhaps never more sharply achieved, though we may wish that he had made up more of it, as he shaped it into myth. The book reads and rereads with a flow of sharp perceptions which, even without documentation, we know come from the very life. The hard surface allows us to indulge our romantic self-pity in secret, to be, with Jake Barnes, tough and decent in spite of our failings, and to imagine ourselves beautifully damned by a world unworthy of us. We read with pleasure, in silent collusion with Hemingway, *aficionados* with a slight consciousness of a little something shameful between us, like the spilling out of the horses in bullfighting.

4

ᦞ FREDERIC HENRY AND THE UNDEFEATED

WHEN SCRIBNER'S published *The Sun Also Rises* on October 22, 1926, Hemingway had already separated from Hadley Richardson, to whom with their three-year-old son, John Hadley Nicanor (namesake of bullfighter Nicanor Villalta), he dedicated the book; and the first phase of Hemingway's career was almost over. The defeated Jake Barnes was to give way to a new undefeated hero, only to recur again in the half-defeated Frederic Henry. "The Undefeated" itself had been written in March, 1925, immediately after Hemingway returned to Paris from Austria exuberant over the acceptance of *In Our Time,* before Pamplona and *The Sun Also Rises.* But Hemingway's undefeated loser was to continue and eventually to triumph in *The Old Man and the Sea,* a type of character running somewhat counter to Nick and Barnes and Henry.

Hemingway had mailed off the manuscript of *The Sun Also Rises* on April 24, 1926. On Sunday, May 16, alone in Madrid, snowed out of the bullfights, he had, as he told Plimpton, written three stories in one day:

> First I wrote "The Killers," which I'd tried to write before and failed. Then after lunch I got in bed to keep warm and wrote "Today Is Friday." I had so much juice I thought maybe I was going crazy and I had about six other stories to write. So I got dressed and walked to Fornos, the old bullfighters' café, and drank coffee and then came back and wrote "Ten Indians." This made me very sad and I drank some brandy and went to sleep.

Later in the spring he had published "Banal Story," probably written late in 1925, a journalistic, torrents-of-spring report about a writer in a cold room, an ad for a literary magazine, and the death by pneumonia of Maera, whose fictive death Hemingway had portrayed from his first impressions of bullfighting. He had spent the summer in Spain, following the fights and thinking of a book on bullfighting, a project first mentioned to Maxwell Perkins of Scribner's in 1925. In July, "To-day Is Friday" had been published as a pamphlet in New Jersey. In December, 1926, two months after *The Sun Also Rises*, "The Undefeated"—already published in German, English, and French—appeared in *The Best Short Stories of 1926*.

In 1927 Hemingway's stories began to appear in American magazines; and he began a long epic novel. In early spring, a ten-day trip through Italy by Model T produced a report for the *New Republic* (May 18) entitled "Italy—1927"—good, oblique journalism to be renamed "Che Ti Dice La Patria" for the coming volume of fiction, an early symptom of the political stirrings of *For Whom the Bell Tolls*, and a stirring of Italian memories for *A Farewell to Arms*. In March "The Killers" was published in *Scribner's Magazine* (also selected for *Best Short Stories of 1927*) and in April, "In Another Country"; in July, "Fifty Grand"; in August, "Hills Like White Elephants," the last of the stories for *Men Without Women* to appear in advance.

The spring of 1927 had seen Hemingway divorced from Hadley Richardson and married to Pauline Pfeiffer, within the Catholic Church. A further manifestation of Hemingway's subterranean Christianity appeared, perhaps a reaction both from Jake Barnes's wistful Catholicism and the rough affirmation of "To-day Is Friday." Hemingway published in Ezra Pound's *Exile* magazine (Spring, 1927) a "poem" that seemed to plead that he had not dropped out of the advance guard after all. Under the misprinted title of "Notheomist Poem," the text reads:

> The Lord is my shepherd, I shall not
> want him for long.

And a footnote explains: "The title 'Neo-Thomist Poem' refers to temporary embracing of church by literary gents—E. H." Hemingway, with his newly embraced Catholic bride, now settled in Key West, Florida—a home in America at last, but at its extreme, fugitive tip.

◦§ §◦

Men Without Women appeared on October 14, 1927, collected from the magazines, with four unpublished stories: two competent ("A Simple Inquiry," "A Pursuit Race"), two splendid ("Ten Indians," "Now I Lay Me"). A month later, on Thanksgiving Day, Hemingway wrote Perkins that he had seventeen chapters, about one third (60,000 words) of what was intended to be "a sort of modern *Tom Jones*." His reading of Fielding, swept into *The Torrents of Spring*, had turned his thoughts to the big epical novel, which he was soon to abandon and later to denounce (in *Death in the Afternoon*): "all bad writers are in love with the epic." He had been trying to write his epic in the first person (obviously not understanding much about epics), and had decided to change everything to third person, having "got tired of the limitations" that had served in *The Sun Also Rises* and would serve again in *A Farewell to Arms*.

Men Without Women, containing some of Hemingway's best stories, nevertheless does not, as a book, equal *In Our Time*. The title merely catches at the masculine deprivation or masculine resentment or masculine independence variously to be found in most of the stories. The title, as Carlos Baker has noted, merely gives an opportune twist to Ford's *"Women and Men,"* the second work in The Three Mountain's Press's series, of which *in our time* had seen the sixth and last. The book balances Hemingway's two emerging modes, which might be called the autobiographical and the observational, roughly the first and the third person between which his "epic" was equivocating, the defeated and the undefeated. In *Men Without Women*, the two modes alternate and engage each other somewhat as two halves of a deck of cards: on the one hand, "In Another Country" and "Now I Lay Me"; on the other, "The Undefeated" and "Fifty Grand." The book begins with "The Undefeated" and ends, like a copy of *In Our Time*, with Nick and symbolic trout streams, in "Now I Lay Me." "The Killers," for all its power, is a hybrid, an observation of the tough world that shifts to a revelation of Nick's inner agony.

The rest of the stories, good and indifferent, fall between, down to "Banal Story," just before the end, which perhaps should have dropped out of sight completely. (Edmund Wilson and W. M. Frohock, however, consider it among Hemingway's best.) "A Simple Enquiry" is an efficient study of a homosexual major, which suffers by comparison with D. H. Lawrence's similar "The Prussian Officer" (published in 1914). "Canary for One" is autobiographical, another and poorer "Out of Season," with a sharp last line. "An Alpine Idyll" and "A Pursuit Race" are unattractive but able stories of isolation and self-destruction.

"Hills Like White Elephants" is better, a study of the destructiveness of the selfish, and a study in Hemingway's ultimate terseness. A man wants his consort to have an abortion so that they can be just as "we were before." The girl knows that the world, with hills like the skin of white elephants, "isn't ours anymore." No matter which way they turn, the man's wish has hurt them beyond repair. Of the story, Hemingway remarked to Plimpton: "I met a girl in Prunier where I'd gone to eat oysters before lunch. I knew she'd had an abortion. I went over and we talked, not about that, but on the way home I thought of the story, skipped lunch, and spent the afternoon writing it." Robert McAlmon indicates (in Knoll's redaction) that a hint of the story had been in Hemingway's mind since the Rapallo days at Pound's, early in 1923, for about five years:

> One night in Rapallo the lot of us were talking of birth control, and spoke of the cruelty of the law which did not allow young un-married women to avoid having an unwanted child. Recalling an incident of college days I told a story of a girl who had managed to have herself taken care of. Her attitude was very casual. "Oh, it was nothing. The doctor just let the air in and a few hours later it was over."

"Two years later," continues McAlmon, with his usual inaccuracy, he saw Hemingway's story "in some magazine": "I didn't see the point of the story and reread it and encountered the phrase 'Let the air in.' Later Hemingway informed me that my remark sug-gested the story." The story is indeed cryptic. The indirection of Hemingway's talk with the girl in Prunier is there; the casual girl of McAlmon's anecdote has turned numb, confronting the casual attitude of her lover; and, of course, there is a great deal more in the story, from white-skinned, fetal oysters to Hemingway himself.

"To-day Is Friday" is Hemingway's first experiment with the drama. Three Roman soldiers are talking in the wineshop of a Hebrew (who is named "George," as is the manager of Henry's lunchroom in "The Killers," written an hour or so before). They discuss the routine crucifixion they have just performed. Heming-way probably intended a shocker, but the play's positive Christianity is empowered by its rough inarticulation. The second soldier, at the lowest rung of understanding, wonders why Christ did not come down off the cross. The first soldier, a good drinker and man of experience, knows "That's not his play." He has illegally "slipped the old spear into him" to end His suffering and reward His bravery. He continues to repeat: "He was pretty good in there to-day." The second soldier calls the first a "regular Christer," and when, as they walk away, the first soldier defends the obsequious George as a "nice fella," the second soldier replies: "Everybody's a nice fella to you to-night." Christ's suffering has taken effect, even at this level of understanding. The third soldier can understand no more than that he has a "gut-ache" and feels "like hell to-night." This is the pagan world, the hellish world, suggesting a spiritual dimension it cannot understand but can partly comprehend. This is Hemingway's earth-bound Christianity, that of Nick—who cannot get beyond "on earth" as he prays, two stories further along—and that of Jake Barnes and Frederic Henry, whose thoughts fly up from their earth-bound souls. It is also Hemingway's first use of Christianity as a symbology for brave Man crucified by the world, as Young says, and as Waldmeir has seen it in *The Old Man and the Sea*.

"The Undefeated" is a big and fine story, the best of Hemingway's bullfighting in fact or fancy, free from the nonsense of *Death in the Afternoon,* surpassing in its thoroughness the picture of Romero in *The Sun Also Rises*. It is in the new mode, projected out and away from the secret autobiography, fiction solidly created from Hemingway's admiration of Manuel Garcia, known as Maera. Indeed, Romero's exhibit of undefeat in his fight with Cohn is no accident, for Romero has a great deal of Maera in him, as well as of Niño de la Palma. Hemingway remembers, in *Death in the Afternoon,* "the last night of feria when Maera fought Alfredo David in the Café Kutz." The aging Manuel Garcia of the story (called "kid" and "Manolo" by his friends) is the first of Hemingway's undefeated losers, connecting his first sketch of Maera with the Old Man of his last novel, whose friend is the boy Manolin.

Hemingway has shifted his attention from the Nicks to the less sensitive friends of the Nicks, those able to live in the world: Bill of "The Three-day Blow," Tommy of "The Light of the World," Bugs of "The Battler," George of "The Killers," Bill Gorton, Romero, Count Mippipoplous, Count Greffi. Not that the essential pattern has changed. The hero is still paired with a friend more able than he, and more worldly wise. But the pair has moved one whole step toward the right, from defeat to undefeat. And the hero is now distinctly a man of lower class and lower intelligence. Garcia is the "little one with the white face"; his friend is the huge Zurito, ten years older, now retired, still the best picador alive. (The real Zurito, in *Death in the Afternoon,* was "the last and one of the greatest of the old-time picadors.") After moments that equal those of the great Belmonte, Garcia, booed by the crowd, and gored, finally kills his bull after five tries. As he goes into oblivion on the operating table, Zurito lets him keep his pigtail, the sign of the fighter, and assures him he was "going great."

It is a fine and moving story, completely presented. The feel and smell and excitement of the bullring are all there, created with remarkable reality from the bullfighter's point of view. The grandeur of undefeat shines from the tawdry surroundings—the heartless manager whose heart can yet light up for a second, the pathetic horses, the useless picadors, the hard crowd up there in the darkness, the jargonal reporter—with the solid Zurito to show that Garcia's dauntless end was unnecessary, and the young Hernandez to show that his beginning was happy. And because the story is cut down to Garcia's size—he cannot read, cannot find words for his thoughts—we have the reality of bullfighting as Hemingway was able to achieve it only occasionally, when he himself did not try to find words to defend all that lies beyond the only defensible area: a man's bravery, skill, and dedication.

The story comes from details firmly caught in Hemingway's imagination, details recorded and imagined in his first report to the Toronto *Star Weekly* and in his first bullfighting sketches—the dark interior from which the bull emerges, the bull turning like a cat, the gored matador and the "kid" who must try five times, only to sit vomiting before the dead bull as the crowd throws things, the "whacked" horses, the little bullfighter pelted and shorn of his pigtail, the fictional Maera first "bumped," then gored and dying on the operating table. All this comes together with the real Maera's great afternoon (in *Death in the Afternoon*) with a dislocated wrist and a bull "made out of cement." All has been re-projected from the point of view of a new imaginary Maera, a man much older, smaller, less skillful, less intelligent than the real Maera, in a triumphant extension of Hemingway's first imaginary projection of him. The young gypsy's excellent banderillaring is also an imaginative transfer of one of Maera's famous skills.

"Fifty Grand," which follows the superb "defeated" interlude of "In Another Country," is another story of an undefeated loser, and again, one of Hemingway's greatest stories. "The Undefeated" is tragic; "Fifty Grand" is comic. It is unique among Hemingway's stories in that the "I" is not the hero but a "character" (Jerry Doyle, the prizefighting hero's trainer). The narrative angle is similar to that of "My Old Man," except that the "I" is neither innocent nor instructed. But his limited intelligence turns all the tawdry details comic and frank, as against the reader's broader perceptions. The picture of the tough world and of Jack Brennan, homebody, worrywart, tightwad, fighter, emerges amusingly and gallantly as Doyle's tight lips give us the wisdom of the ring as if it were the wisdom of the world: "Jack got a good hand coming down through the crowd. Jack is Irish and the Irish always get a pretty good hand. An Irishman don't draw in New York like a Jew or an Italian but they always get a good hand."

Doyle's observations and omissions constantly give marvelous flashes of character and detail to solidify the boxing world, in which the champion moves:

> "What do you make it?" Jack asked the fellows who were weighing.
> "One hundred and forty-three pounds," the fat man who was weighing said.

Something in the colloquial rhythm, something in the weighty reply, something in the narrator's simple assumption that we know all about "weighing" and the fat man who does it, makes that solid flesh immortal.

This is the world that Hemingway first attempted in high school in "A Matter of Colour," and in his postgraduate course at the Chicago gym. But unlike the high-school story, "Fifty Grand" turns a tricked ending into a supreme test of wits and courage. The brave and amusing Brennan, the classic boxer who can out-gouge anyone in the clinches, the homebody who fights for a living, is to be seen again in Harry Morgan of *To Have and Have Not,* the buccaneer alone against a buccaneering world. Jack Brennan, as with the bullfighter before and Morgan after, was modeled on a man Hemingway admired: Jack Britton, who, as Hemingway was to tell Lillian Ross, "kept on his toes and moved around and never let them hit him solid."

❦ ❧

Underneath the growing manuscript of Hemingway's modern *Tom Jones,* his third-person observation of the world, the old inner cry persisted. Early in March, 1928, Hemingway began his final telling of the story of the nurse in Milan, dropping the epic completely. He began *A Farewell to Arms* in Paris, continued during the spring and summer in Key West, wrote a good deal of the book in Havana, went on in Arkansas and Kansas City, and finished the first draft in Wyoming in August, six months later. In another five months, on January 22, 1929, he wrote Perkins that revision was complete. In May, *A Farewell to Arms* began to appear monthly in *Scribner's Magazine,* Hemingway changing galley proof all the way. Book proof arrived in Paris on June 5. Hemingway mailed it back on June 24, finally achieving a "new and better ending" after thirty-nine rewritings. Scribner's published it on September 27, 1929.

A Farewell to Arms is a welling up of the concern with birth and death with which Hemingway had begun *In Our Time,* together with his surrogate hero, Nick, wounded into separate peace, man against a senseless world. The Caesarian delivery of Hemingway's second son, Patrick, at the end of June, 1928—when the first draft was nearing completion—colored the Caesarian (and the paternal anxiety) with which Hemingway ends the book, and with which he had dealt in the first story of *In Our Time.* His father's suicide during the rewriting underlined the tragic, as his "Introduction" to the 1948 edition was to reveal:

> I remember all these things happening and all the places we lived in and the fine times and the bad times we had that year. But much more vividly I remember living in the book and making up what happened in it every day. Making the country and the people and the things that happened I was happier than I had ever been. Each day I read the book through from the beginning to the point where I went on writing and each day I stopped when I was still going good and when I knew what would happen next. The fact that the book was a tragic one did not make me unhappy since I believed that life was a tragedy and knew it could only have one end. But finding you were able to make something up; to create truly enough so that it made you happy to read it; and to do this every day you worked was something that gave a greater pleasure than any I had ever known. Beside it nothing else mattered.

Hemingway's "making up" what happened is frequently a re-capturing of country traversed before. Nick, wounded and propped against the church, and his friend Rinaldi became Lieutenant Frederic Henry and his roommate Rinaldi, now non-combatants, ambulance officer and surgeon. The unnamed soldier under bombardment at Fossalta who prays "Oh Jesus Christ get me out of here . . . please, please, please . . . I'll do anything you say" becomes young Henry, who, when blown up at night, says "Oh God get me out of here" and who prays, later, when his wife is dying: "Please, please, please don't let her die. God please make her not die. I'll do anything you say if you don't let her die."

63

Hemingway's Italian retreat from Caporetto, which he knew only by report, revives the Greek retreat from Adrianople (as Malcolm Cowley has detected), and revives it in the language both of his Toronto dispatch and of his revision for *in our time*. The Maritza River that "was running yellow almost up to the bridge" becomes the Tagliamento flooded "close under the wooden planking." The Thracian road is now Italian. Here is *in our time*: ". . . carts loaded with everything they owned. The old men and women, soaked through, walked along keeping the cattle moving. . . . The women and children were in the carts, crouched with mattresses, mirrors, sewing machines, bundles." Remembering other details reported to Toronto ("This main stream is being swelled from all the back country"—"Chickens dangle by their feet from the carts"), Hemingway now re-creates the Italian retreat:

> In the night many peasants had joined the column from the roads of the country and in the column there were carts loaded with household goods; there were mirrors projecting up between mattresses, and chickens and ducks tied to carts. There was a sewing-machine on the cart ahead of us in the rain. They had saved the most valuable things. On some carts the women sat huddled from the rain and others walked beside the carts keeping as close to them as they could.

As we have noted, the Thracian retreat taught Hemingway to saturate disaster with rain, as he does throughout the book.

Lieutenant Henry is almost an anthology of Lieutenant Nick (not to mention Jake Barnes and the "joke" Italian front). "In bed I lay me down my head," thinks Henry; and he has trouble sleeping without a light, prays hopelessly, has faith only during the fears of the night. He has a skull fracture, shuts off his thoughts, says of the war: "I'll tell you about it if I ever get it straight in my head." He is wounded in knee and calf; he exercises on machines in a Milan hospital to which he walks daily, looking in the shops; he knows his medals are undeserved; and, later, Italians shout at him, as at Nick, "*A basso gli ufficiali!*" The Italian major's advice to Nick sounds like an unheeded warning against Henry's tragedy: a man must not marry, for, "if he is to lose everything, he should not place himself in a position to lose that." As many have noted, Henry repeats Nick's very first words about making a "separate peace."

Of course, the story is significantly different from Nick's, and from the one first sketched about the nurse in *in our time*. Henry, an architectural student in Italy, joins the Italian ambulance corps because he can speak Italian. His roommate, Rinaldi, introduces him to Catherine Barkley, a Scotch nurse of the British Voluntary Aid Detachment. She carries the riding crop of a childhood fiancé recently killed in France. Henry makes advances; she slaps him, embraces him, says they will lead a strange life. "What the hell," thinks Henry. He is wounded by an explosion of a mortar shell while eating macaroni and cheese in an ambulance drivers' dugout. Catherine transfers to the Milan hospital, Henry falls in love in earnest, and Catherine becomes pregnant.

Henry returns to the front (October 4, 1917—Hemingway has again, as in *The Sun Also Rises,* put the story one year ahead of his personal life). He is just in time for the Italian retreat from Caporetto, from which, his trucks and men lost one by one, he finally deserts by leaping into the Tagliamento when battle police try to shoot him as a spy. In civilian clothes, he joins Catherine in the Italian Alps, from which they escape to Switzerland, rowing all night across a stormy lake. They wait for the baby, finally delivered, dead, as Catherine dies, and Henry walks back to the hotel, alone, in the rain.

Robert Penn Warren, triangulating from Hemingway's other work, has admirably described what this is supposed to mean. The story does catch, as Warren says, the long rumble of disintegrating Christian and social faith that reached a crescendo in World War I. Henry wants some kind of faith like that of the priest in the officers' mess, who comes from mountains where a man may love God, and religion "is not a dirty joke." Henry will find his faith in the religion of love, and will learn, as the priest says, to sacrifice and to serve. Henry learns, says Warren, that personal love is doomed by all the accidents of a blackguard universe, that the whole is "just a dirty trick" after all—"But this is not to deny the value of the effort, or to deny the value of the discipline, the code, the stoic endurance, the things that make it true—or half true—that 'nothing ever happens to the brave.' "

Unfortunately, this does not fit Henry, as it does fit Manuel and Hemingway's other undefeated losers. Henry is not wholly one of the "disciplined": he finds that his officering is first unnecessary, then ineffective, then meaningless. Even the disciplined Rinaldi goes glum, his surgical skill no longer adequate protection from the diseased world. Henry is not one of the brave: he knows his batting is only average. Henry may have learned "the value of effort," though Hemingway is far from intent on the demonstration. Henry does say, "It has only happened to me like that once," as he looks back on the story he is telling, exactly as Nick looks back in "Now I Lay Me," when all was long ago and he has never married. In this single remark, Henry indicates that he has learned the full value of what he has lost. But Warren's "effort" can mean only the effort to make love last, which is something different from "the discipline, the code, the stoic endurance." James Light and others who laud Henry's stoicism merely extend Warren's misreading.

Henry is not one of the undefeated, nor is he one of the defeated so sweetly drawn in the alienated Nick and the sleepless Nick, so commendably drawn in Barnes. Henry is still capable of action, and his own action defeats him, contrary, I think, to what Hemingway intends and Warren reads. Jake Barnes is a rugged name and man, whom war has prepared for Brett's slaughter. Nick Adams has the very name of Man, but war has nicked him and knocked him out. And in his defeat he eventually invites, I believe, a faint sneer from his creator, who calls him a condescending "Nicholas." "Frederic Henry" has the same faint scorn in it, the faintly effeminate ring already heard in the "Henry" on the lips of the Doctor's wife, in "Henry" Braddocks and in the chauffeur Henry of *The Sun Also Rises*, and in other recurrent Henrys. As Young suggests, Hemingway may have adapted the name from Stephen Crane, whose own frequent and slightly patronized Henrys culminate in Henry Fleming (a name virtually the reverse of "Frederic Henry") of *The Red Badge of Courage*. Hemingway may have seen the name as a kind of personal anagram, half-conscious and self-accusatory: "Henry" compressed from "Hemingway," with "Frederic" another first name calling for defense. We will see the same thing in the naming of Francis Macomber—in a story that may, as Young suggests, derive its plot from Crane's *Red Badge*. Even a *k* on "Frederic" would have toughened it slightly. Is Henry's name "Frederico Enrico or Enrico Federico?"—an Italian messmate asks (Rinaldi calls him "Federico," without the *r*). To be sure, Hemingway may have been thinking of Frederic Manning, soldier and avant-garde writer in Paris, whose *The Middle Parts of Fortune* (published in 1929, contemporaneously with *A Farewell to Arms*) Hemingway was to read each year on the anniversary of Hemingway's (and Henry's) wounding. Again, we may think of *Henry IV*, whence big-game hunter Wilson's brave motto, and even of Frederick the Great. But Hemingway and the modern world have undermined the glory in those names. "Frederic Henry" is a strange name for a modern hero, alongside the Nicks and Jakes and Jacks.

Hemingway's uncertainty, uncontrolled because not thoroughly understood, follows Henry to the end. In spite of feminine shadows, Henry is an astounding lover, a man's man, well-liked by barkeep and count, able at doing "those things that gave you a false sense of soldiering"; slightly contemptuous of the real soldier, slightly contemptuous of his own job, too, yet disappointed to see how well it runs without him. He is an officer—an officer in an army not an army, somewhat behind the lines of a secondary front: in the war but not of it. There is with Henry, from the beginning, a sense of uneasiness, of disillusion, about one's role.

There is, indeed, a strange confusion of male and female which, though poetic and almost choreographic, probably goes deeper than Hemingway knew. In the beginning, cartridge boxes on the belts of muddy troops "bulged forward under the capes so that the men, passing on the road, marched as though they were six months gone with child"; and at the end, Catherine out walking on the road "did not look big with the cape . . . ." In the beginning, we have Henry and Rinaldi, his roommate who kisses him and calls him "baby" in the Italian manner; in the end, Catherine and Henry. The book begins, on the masculine side of the dance, as if a married couple and not a group of men—indeed as if a wife—were looking out at the war: "In the late summer of that year we lived in a house in a village that looked across the river and the plain to the mountains. . . . Troops went by the house and down the road. . . ." The second chapter begins with identical domesticity, even more cloistered: "we" are now living "in a house in Glorizia that had a fountain and many thick shady trees in a walled garden and a wistaria vine purple on the side of the house." This is indistinguishable from the domesticity of Catherine and Henry at the end: "That fall the snow came very late. We lived in a brown wooden house in the pine trees on the side of the mountain . . . ." At the end, the magic of the mountains, as Carlos Baker says, is at work. But at the beginning, the untutored reader may be surprised when he finally comes upon the soft-voiced narrator looking at the snow out of the window of a bawdy house, an officer drinking with another officer. At the beginning, whether we like it or not, the anonymous Frederic Henry sounds very much like a woman.

At the end, when Henry is supposed to be disciplined and stoic and filled with valuable effort, we find that he is in fact unmanned by Catherine, defeated by Catherine, as Theodore Bardacke has pointed out, in his "Hemingway's Women," just as surely as Barnes is unmanned vis-à-vis Brett. Hemingway's basic distrust of women has unstrung his lyre. The nurse who threw him over will not wholly convert into the lady true unto death. Catherine of the long blond hair, which first catches Henry's eye, which tents their kisses in bed, is not so womanly as Hemingway seems to suppose. She is uncomfortably similar to the sleek British Brett of Jake's hospital tour. Young has already noted their similar backgrounds as nurses with lovers killed in the war. Catherine is also narrow of hip; she wants to bob her hair, to forget maternity. She makes Henry her plaything, having him grow a beard (on which he asks instructions), wanting him to grow his hair a little longer: ". . . and I could cut mine and we'd be just alike only one of us blonde and one of us dark." Make me a boy again just for tonight! She wants "to be you too"; she wants "us to be all mixed up." She does not really want him to go skiing with the men; and Henry replies, "I won't ever go away. . . . I'm no good when you're not there. I haven't any life at all any more." When Catherine says that she will cut her hair when she is thin again, and become "a fine new and different girl" for him to fall in love with:

> "Hell," I said. "I love you enough now. What do you want to do? Ruin me?"
> "Yes. I want to ruin you."
> "Good," I said, "That's what I want too."

What Henry thinks in his last phase, he does not record. He tries not to think. We do learn that the beard makes him self-conscious in the shadow-boxing mirror at the gym, and that it makes him seem in the hospital mirror "a fake doctor with a beard." But he likes it; it gives him "something to do." Catherine likes it: "It looks so stiff and fierce and it's very soft and a great pleasure." It is a perfect symbol for Henry's disguised effeminacy, fierce yet false, really soft to please a woman. Henry is much the war-numbed Nick, also much the man forbearing with a woman with child, giving and serving at last as the priest said he would. But he is unmanned nevertheless; and the beard (as with Hemingway's own) makes a compensation too obvious. Awake one night, he hears Catherine, also lying awake, mention her first "craziness." He lies "awake for quite a long time thinking about things and watching Catherine sleeping, the moonlight on her face."

Life with the beautiful Catherine does arouse uneasy thought.

She remains something of a puzzle to the reader. Edmund Wilson and Malcolm Cowley and others have found her unsatisfactory, a masculine daydream on paper; and Carlos Baker has only called up other unsatisfactory heroines in her defense. Cowley, indeed, has hit the startling truth when he says that she is credible only at the beginning—"in her near madness." Actually, Catherine, who continues to say that she is "all right now" and no longer "crazy," retains uncomfortable touches of madness—among which, her very protestations—until pregnancy takes its benign effect. Hemingway records a clinical history he seems not to understand, just as he fails to see through the twilight of his hero.

Catherine is afraid of the rain, because she sees herself dead in it. On the other hand, she is strangely blithe, living in the moment, careless of contraception, of marriage, of pregnancy, of going A.W.O.L., of Henry's deserting, of danger, of crossing a stormy lake with little concern. She has no religion, none of Henry's feeling that perhaps one should. She goes into sudden reverie, thinking her first sexual experience the same as her madness:

> She came back from wherever she had been.
> . . . .
> "I had a very fine little show and I'm all right now. You see I'm not mad and I'm not gone off. It's only a little sometimes."

When she tells Henry she is pregnant, she suddenly goes "away a long way" and comes "back from wherever she had been"—a phrase to knell ominously at the end when, after temporary anesthetic, she "came back from a long way away."

And with all the cheeriness, she is paranoid: "We work very hard but no one trusts us"—"there's only us two and in the world there's all the rest of them. If anything comes between us we're gone and then they have us." This, the two "alone against the others," Henry eventually takes for his own, now needing Catherine to keep him from fears of the night. Henry and Hemingway take this strange insulation of Catherine's as "so much courage" that the world must finally break her. To be sure, Catherine is attractive scene by scene, and perfectly credible, with her ability to make a cot a home, her daintiness of nightgown, her pleasant spirits; but she remains ephemeral because neither Henry nor Hemingway can add her scenes accurately. Hemingway has unwittingly, I think, written the story that also defeated F. Scott Fitzgerald in *Tender is the Night,* though Fitzgerald at least knew what he was attempting: the story of a man unmanned in trying to serve the charming fey.

Perhaps the real source of our uneasiness (and of Hemingway's) is Henry himself. Hemingway writes a story about manhood and self-respect lost for a love that ends in death, and he thinks he has written of a transcendent love crushed by a meaningless world, and of a man learning to take the ultimate loss. Henry is ruined by woman, not by the world; and he is enough of the man of action to be vaguely haunted by a mistake neither he nor Hemingway can admit, though they suggest its pressure.

For Henry's "separate peace," contrary to several distinguished opinions, is not that announced by young Nick to his Rinaldi. Nick had been joking, as he notes with satisfaction that the battle is succeeding on up the street and that the stretchers soon will come. He and Rinaldi are no longer "patriots"—apparently the term, in the slightly anarchistic Italian army, for the eager soldier, the military apple-polisher of any army. Like swallow-tailed ambassadors, Nick and Rinaldi have made a "separate peace," in a phrase then current among the uneasy allies. Nick is joking because they have been knocked out of the war and out of patriotism by enemy gunfire. Their peace has been not at all of their own making. Lieutenant Henry's peace, however, is of his own making. He is hale and on his feet. He deserts a disintegrating army, angry, to be sure, and with considerable provocation. But he has taken the action. Now, in civilian clothes, he is in a train with some scornful aviators (shades of Jake Barnes!). They leave. He does not want to read the paper: "I was going to forget the war. I had made a separate peace. I felt damned lonely. . . ."

Henry has deserted, saving himself through anger and for love. He knows that the unpatriotic Piani will return to the unit, more constant though with much less danger. Henry's conscience bothers him, but soon Catherine absorbs even this:

> It was clouding over outside and the lake was darkening.
> "I wish we did not always have to live like criminals," I said.
> "Darling, don't be that way. You haven't lived like a criminal very long. And we never live like criminals. We're going to have a fine time."
> "I feel like a criminal. I've deserted from the army."
> "Darling, *please* be sensible. It's not deserting from the army. It's only the Italian army."
> I laughed. "You're a fine girl. Let's get back into bed. I feel fine in bed."

Henry's symbolic resignation from society, which we accept with lessened qualms, Warren points out, because it is only the Italian army, leaves Henry the misgivings he can forget only in Catherine's arms. Like the war-numbed Nick, he stops his mind from thinking; but with Nick it was horror, and with Henry it is guilt. "Abstract words such as glory, honor, courage, or hallow were obscene beside the concrete names of villages, . . . the numbers of regiments and the dates." True. But as Henry attempts to reject the society that has mouthed the words (and has kept paying his sight-drafts without question), he cannot forget, as Hemingway himself could not, that he bore no honored nor courageous number, that he was only a pseudo-officer, that his medals were slightly spurious. Henry is enough of an undefeated man of action to leave him, and us, uneasy about his defeated inaction at the end. Catherine's death, which leaves him utterly alone in the rain, cannot quite weigh as an indictment of the world and its wars, nor as a lesson for Henry, nor as a splendor of irrational ironies, hardly even as a tragedy of young life wasted in the world's tangle—the *Romeo and Juliet* that Hemingway and Carlos Baker have hoped it to be. The meaning simply drifts away, uncertainly, in the rain.

But the book has a poetry that almost holds it together: *A Farewell to Arms*—the lonely, lyric *A*, the heraldic diction. The title is poetic, indeed, being also the title of a poem by the Elizabethan, George Peele, who regretfully bids both the arms of glory and the arms of love farewell, as Philip Young and Jerome L. Mazzaro have pointed out. Professor Harry Levin has thought that the title came from Richard Lovelace. And though Lovelace can show no phrase even close, no such pun on the arms of love and war, Hemingway's sweet goodbye would certainly have been stronger and truer if, indeed, his Henry had flown to Warre and Armes, and not from them, if he had tried to rejoin his scattered unit though a Hell of carabinieri should bar the way, though he should have been disgracefully shot, knowing that he could not love his Dear so much loved he not Honour more.

But the song goes flat only after the flight to Switzerland, and we realize that a peg must have slipped unnoticed. Minute by minute, the song is, in Warren's word, hypnotic, as it sings of what it is like to be in a war in a world adrift, and to know the excitements of love made reckless in consequence. The march of the seasons, chapter by chapter, the ominous march of the rain, the two alone in the night against the flashes of war, yes, it is good:

That night a bat flew into the room through the open door that led onto the balcony and through which we watched the night over the roofs of the town. It was dark in our room except for the small light of the night over the town and the bat was not frightened but hunted in the room as though he had been outside. We lay and watched him and I do not think he saw us because we lay so still. After he went out we saw a searchlight come on and watched the beam move across the sky and then go off and it was dark again. A breeze came in the night and we heard the men of the anti-aircraft gun on the next roof talking.

Hemingway has in fact used poetry itself for his poetic effects: Henry quotes Marvell's famous couplet (learned from the man who made it famous, T. S. Eliot, as Donna Gerstenberger has shown and Hemingway himself has indicated in *Death in the Afternoon*):

> But at my back I always hear
> Time's wingèd chariot hurrying near.

And toward the end, the lovers feel "as though something were hurrying us and we could not lose any time together." The little pre-Elizabethan lyric about the western wind and the small rain and love's arms is even more intricately suffused through Henry's thoughts of Catherine during the retreat, as Charles R. Anderson has shown in his "Hemingway's Other Style." Hemingway's characteristic reiteration of word, phrase, and picture are beautifully and darkly expanded so that the essential lyric cry of self is braided with harmonics from beginning to end. And the construction is nicely balanced: "pregnant" troops at the beginning, pregnant Catherine at the end; statues in the hospital as Henry meets Catherine, Catherine dead in the hospital like a statue, as he leaves her.

As with the exposition, so with the scenes—Catherine in the red plush room, Henry and the pompous doctors:

"Do you want to keep your knee, young man?"
"No," I said.
"What?"
"I want it cut off." I said, "so I can wear a hook on it."

The secondary characterizations are perfect: Rinaldi, and Valentini the other surgeon, and Ferguson, and Count Greffi (one of Ezra Pound's old men with "beautiful manners"), and the wonderful Italian ambulance drivers—the kind of idiomatic portraiture Hemingway first struck in "Out of Season," and continued in "Now

I Lay Me." The whole retreat from Caporetto is as vivid as anything Hemingway ever wrote, subtly touched with reminders of love sacred and profane, the soldier's only solace (as Anderson says): the harlot of the fluttering tongue, the frightened virgins, the inexplicit dream of Catherine. The book is full of the kind of writing and seeing that would make its author happy every day: the "sudden interiors of houses that had lost a wall through shelling"; troops that "moved smoothly, almost supernaturally" over a bridge, before Henry sees that they are on bicycles; or this: "I sat up straight and as I did so something inside my head moved like the weights on a doll's eyes and it hit me inside in back of my eyeballs."

Yet, as Edmund Wilson said some time ago and I am surprised to discover, *A Farewell to Arms* is a lesser book than *The Sun Also Rises,* even a lesser love story. The romantic cry is not so true, nor even so sad, since Henry leaves us trying to blame the world for private deficiencies as well as for Catherine's death, and a still, small Tiresian voice warns us against trying to smoke the bounder out. The little major of "In Another Country" was completely convincing, as was the unwarranted death of his young wife. His is a world of some cruel whim, and his cry that one should not marry and expose oneself is right from the heart. But Henry is so unmanned by his wife, as the major is not, that toward the end we can almost read a resentful cryptogram, to the effect that men can remain undefeated only without women.

5

◄§ BULLS, AND WINNERS
WITH NOTHING

IN MAY, 1929, with *A Farewell to Arms* completed and success won, Hemingway published a clear symptom of the writer's endemic fear that he has said his say. Mr. Lee Wilson Dodd had questioned the narrowness of Hemingway's interests ("the bullfighters, bruisers, touts, gunmen, professional soldiers, prostitutes, hard drinkers, dope fiends"), and the value of his artistry, in reviewing *Men Without Women* for the *Saturday Review of Literature* (November 19, 1927). Hemingway's "Valentine" in the *Little Review*, his last foray into verse, replies to Dodd and all his critical friends, especially, as Robert P. Weeks notes, Joseph Wood Krutch, two of whose phrases appear in the poem. Hemingway accuses Dodd and the other critics of waiting to pounce on him at the first sign of decay—a point Dodd does not make in any way. But *Death in the Afternoon* and *Winner Take Nothing* were to demonstrate that Hemingway's big creative burst was over. His fame was growing (as was his family— Gregory was born, also by Caesarian, in the fall of 1931). Interruptions at Key West were constant. Hemingway had indeed temporarily written himself out, and he was entering a period of depression curiously coincidental with the great Depression of the thirties.

Hemingway had first gone to Spain to see the bullfights sometime after April 1, 1923, an important date, especially since both Carlos Baker and Charles Fenton assume, from Hemingway's own misleading remarks, that Hemingway was in Spain in 1922. To be sure, he had landed at Vigo, Spain, in mid-December, 1921, proceeding to Paris by train. The Toronto *Star Weekly* had published Hemingway's description of Vigo, his first report, on February 18, 1922. But this trip did not count. Hemingway's *Star Weekly* story of October 20, 1923 (which both Baker and Fenton mention), states that "it was very exciting sitting out in front of a cafe your first day in Spain," and that "it was the first bull fight I ever saw." Henry ("Mike") Strater, illustrator of Pound's *Cantos* and of Hemingway's portrait from which the *in our time* woodcut was copied, had drawn a map of the right places in Madrid for Hemingway and "Mike" (a disguise for Robert McAlmon, and not the "Mike Strater" of Fenton's misreading of the news story).[1] "It was spring in Paris," wrote Hemingway, "and everything looked just a little too beautiful."

His *Little Review* sketches had just appeared, on April 1, 1923. So off he went to Spain to try the bullfights that were to lead first to *The Sun Also Rises* and then to *Death in the Afternoon*.

Hemingway had first mentioned a big bullfighting book—to do for the bull ring, with "wonderful pictures," what Doughty's *Arabia Deserta* had done for the desert—on April 15, 1925: in his very first letter to Maxwell Perkins, before the Pamplona outing and *The Sun Also Rises*. With *A Farewell to Arms* off his hands in June, 1929, Hemingway went again to Spain, having been in America during the 1928 season ("Wine of Wyoming," published two years later, comes from this year of Al Smith's election campaign, as Carlos Baker has noted). Hemingway began *Death in the Afternoon* in the fall of 1929, in almost exact coincidence with the Wall Street crash. In the fall of 1930, hunting in Wyoming, he reports the manuscript complete, except for two chapters. In November, 1930, a bad automobile accident put him in the hospital at Billings, Montana, where he recovered slowly, and where he derived "The Gambler, the Nun, and the Radio," to be published three years later. By August, 1931, he reports his glossary complete; and toward the end of November, his last chapter. On January 13, 1932, he had finished revising. Scribner's published *Death in the Afternoon* on September 26, 1932.

The book has been hailed as the bible and Baedeker of bullfighting. It has been excavated for Hemingway's famous literary dicta, particularly about writing truly and not "faking," a charge weighed against imperfect bullfighters throughout the book. It contains the lushest of Hemingway's prose, some memorable portraits and anecdotes, and some beautiful pictures. But it also shows a decay, an uncertainty of stance, and more than a little of the fakery that Hemingway denounces. "No. It is not enough of a book, but still there were a few things to be said. There were a few practical

[1] Mr. Strater, now a director of the museum at Ogunquit, Maine, throws some light on the question in a letter to me, dated August 18, 1962:

The next summer, I believe (1923) was when Hem first went to Spain. By accident, I had stayed in Madrid at a pension for bullfighters (I liked the bullfighters, but not the spectators). I made a little map of the Puerta del Sol area, to help him find the pension. McAlmon was married to a wealthy English girl, and financed the trip to Spain, himself and Hem.
. . . No "Mike" went to Spain with Hem.

things to be said." So Hemingway closes. And he has summed it up with disturbing accuracy, in a stagy flourish. Hemingway, successful, self-conscious, and worried, has been drinking too much, as he all too clearly tells us. Once, about ten years ago in Pamplona, he tells us, with some friends who had never seen a bullfight (the very cast for *The Sun Also Rises,* I like to think), he "had spoken of the brilliance, the art, the and so forth of bullfighting at great length. I held forth a long time, stimulated to eloquence by two or three absinthes at the Café Kutz . . . ." Much of the book sounds exactly this bibulous. He and "the old lady who winningly serves as his tuning fork" (in Carlos Baker's view) sit in the Café Fornos as Hemingway clowns his way along, sometimes mocking his subject, sometimes taking it seriously:

> But, you say, there is very little conversation in this book. Why isn't there more dialogue? What we want in a book by this citizen is people talking; that is all he knows how to do and now he doesn't do it. The fellow is no philosopher, no savant, an incompetent zoologist, he drinks too much and cannot punctuate readily and now he has stopped writing dialogue. Some one ought to put a stop to him. He is bull crazy. Citizen, perhaps you are right. Let us have a little dialogue.

Again the torrents of spring have caught him. He cannot face his subject soberly and steadily because this would be to join the world of the mind as opposed to the world of sensation. He is indeed no philosopher, and he cannot play the savant without embarrassment. Again he resorts inappropriately to digressions and intrusions on the pattern of Henry Fielding.

Hemingway's theories frequently will not bear inspection, as when he tries to excuse the spilling out of the horses as dramatic and comic, recording "truly what you really felt, rather than what you were supposed to feel." Once, however, he does get it straight:

> Killing cleanly and in a way which gives you aesthetic pleasure and pride has always been one of the greatest enjoyments of a part of the human race. . . . One of its greatest pleasures, aside from the purely aesthetic ones, such as wing shooting, and the ones of pride, such as difficult game stalking, where it is the disproportionately increased importance of the fraction of a moment that it takes for the shot that furnishes the emotion, is the feeling of rebellion against death which comes from its administering. Once you accept the rule of death thou shalt not kill is an easily and a naturally obeyed commandment. But when a man is still in rebellion against death he has pleasure in taking

to himself one of the Godlike attributes; that of giving it. This is one of the most profound feelings in those men who enjoy killing. These things are done in pride and pride, of course, is a Christian sin, and a pagan virtue. But it is pride which makes the bullfight and true enjoyment of killing which makes the great matador.

Hemingway sees the truth, within his limits; and he reveals himself. He cannot accept a life that includes death. He remains in rebellion against the injustice of such an arrangement, even unto the last moment when he administered to himself.

The fallacy in Hemingway's position remains obvious. It produces the expertise, the ostentation of lore, the careful analysis of technique, which can cover defects far larger than Hemingway's. Reduce everything to skill and aesthetics, and one can justify any inhumanity. And the wobble in Hemingway's apologetics suggests what a great deal of his creative work suggests, where his sympathies are not embarrassed by thought: he has a sense of justice after all. "A writer without a sense of justice and of injustice would be better off editing the year book of a school for exceptional children than writing novels," he was to say to Plimpton. But in *Death in the Afternoon,* his moral and professional uncertainty are painfully apparent. His voice continually goes hollow as he solemnizes—in a kind of sedate parody of Spanish idiom—over whether this or that fighter "gives the emotion." Although his style swells to authentic beauty when, once or twice, he describes what the ballet of death does to fighter and spectator as the sword goes in, it also meanders, and it falls into a new grammatical laxity.

For a writer who, as MacLeish's poem says, "whittled a style for his time from a walnut stick," *Death in the Afternoon* is badly "unwhittled." The colloquial redundancies, wonderful in a Jack Brennan, are simply redundancies in the remarks of a well-whittled author. A convenient example is the common colloquial seepage of *would have* from main clause to *if*-clause: "If I *would have* gone, I *would have* seen" for "If I *had* gone . . . ." One probably cannot find this construction in Hemingway's earlier prose. It appears oddly once in *A Farewell to Arms,* in a speech of the Scottish Catherine (reported, to be sure, by the American Frederic): "He could have had anything he wanted if I *would have* known." But Hemingway's new garrulousness in *Death in the Afternoon* several times carries him off his guard: "I was not able to write anything about it for five years—and I wish I *would have* waited ten"; I know that if I *would have* been away from Spain . . ."; "if he *would have* had the cold, passionate, wolf-courage of Belmonte there could never have been a greater bullfighter."

Small redundancies reflect larger ones. On one page Hemingway explains the "master" horn; on the next he writes: "Nearly every bull has one horn that he prefers to use more than the other and this horn is called the master horn." Hemingway, in love with Spain, has fallen into the pidgin English of his fictional Italians and Spaniards, into what he here describes as the bullfighter's "Aragonese sort of baby talk dialect," the "childish language" of a "simple peasantry." And his own stature and his subject shrink accordingly toward the false and childish: "if the period of apprenticeship is of the proper duration and if the apprentice has good fortune."

Hemingway's language often seems a kind of cape to protect him from his subject. He continually breaks away in embarrassment, as at the end of this excellent depiction:

> Cagancho is a gypsy, subject to fits of cowardice, altogether without integrity, who violates all the rules, written and unwritten, for the conduct of a matador but who, when he receives a bull that he has confidence in, and he has confidence in them very rarely, can do things which all bullfighters do in a way they have never been done before and sometimes standing absolutely straight with his feet still, planted as though he were a tree, with the arrogance and grace that gypsies have and of which all other arrogance and grace seems an imitation, moves the cape spread full as the pulling jib of a yacht before the bull's muzzle so slowly that the art of bullfighting, which is only kept from being one of the major arts because it is impermanent, in the arrogant slowness of his veronicas becomes, for the seeming minutes that they endure, permanent. That is the worst sort of flowery writing, but it is necessary to try to give the feeling. . . .

A more interesting defect, however, is Hemingway's virtual fakery of the facts. He begins his book by mentioning that Gertrude Stein's admiration of Joselito had first interested him in bullfighting; and Joselito becomes one of the ideal fighters of the book. But although Hemingway twice mentions the date of Joselito's death, May 16, 1920, one is very much surprised to discover that Hemingway, arriving only in the spring of 1923, never saw him. One would never suspect that Hemingway was not there: "Watching Joselito was like reading about D'Artagnan when you were a boy. You did not worry about him finally because he had too much ability." And so with Manuel Granero, "killed in the ring in

Madrid in 1922 . . . by a Veragua bull that lifted him once, then tossed him against the wood of the foot of the barrera and never left him until the horn had broken up the skull as you might break a flowerpot. He was a fine-looking boy who had studied the violin. . . ." And again: "The best swordsmen in my time were Manuel Vare, called Varelito, probably the best killer of my generation, Antonio de la Haba . . . . Not yet recovered from the effects of a horn wound received the year before, [Varelito] was unable to kill with his old style in the April fair in Seville in 1922. . . ." This continues into an anecdote of Varelito's death, told with all the vividness of a witness. And the same is true of one of the best anecdotes in the book, of how El Gallo, after dedicating first to one friend then another "the last bull of his life," during one of his several final retirements, walked toward the bull, eyed him, then turned to his brother Joselito and said, "Kill him for me, José. Take him for me. I don't like the way he looks at me."

Hemingway's disdain of pedantry has combined with an imagination that makes little distinction among personal experience, the anecdotes of others, and its own fictive creation. *Death in the Afternoon* is factual, I do not doubt. But the book nevertheless indicates, again, that Hemingway's imagination, "making it all up," would not, and perhaps sometimes could not—as with Nick's trout streams—distinguish what he had seen from what he had imagined. Witness Jake Barnes: "I read the Turgenieff. I knew that now, reading it in the oversensitized state of my mind after much too much brandy, I would remember it somewhere, and afterward it would seem as though it had really happened to me. I would always have it." One suspects that this phenomenon, of no especial relevance for Barnes in the story, is true of Ernest Hemingway. When Barnes, "quite drunk," starts reading the story, it seems new, although he had read it before, and "the country became very clear and the feeling of pressure in my head seemed to loosen." The phrasing makes a peculiar parallel with "the country" Hemingway claims to have "made up" while actually describing with fair accuracy the surroundings of Seney, Michigan. "Memory, of course, is never true," as Hemingway says, truly, in *Death in the Afternoon*. Hemingway's discrimination between journalism and fiction is not so clear as he and Carlos Baker liked to think. In *Death in the Afternoon,* he confuses anecdote with observation; and though he does not falsify the record, certainly, he is strangely misleading for one pursuing the truth.

His close friendship with El Gallo, Joselito's older brother, the Raphael of the fine last chapter, accounts for some of the blurring. The stories surrounding the two brothers, along with those of other fighters of the period, often heard, often told in the winy haze, have joined what Hemingway has seen, becoming a personal mythology of the golden days. El Gallo—who once, when asked what he did for exercise, said that he smoked cigars—remains the liveliest personality of the book. Hemingway knew him and loved him; and Hemingway pored over the pictures that were to give his book its final stability until they became, as his captions show, a part of his visual imagination, so real indeed that Hemingway's absences seem trivial as the reader gazes at El Gallo dedicating the last bull of his life. Watching Joselito must indeed have been like reading about D'Artagnan, even if you yourself had never seen him; and Hemingway moves from this hypnotic perception into one of his two best descriptions of the emotional power in bullfighting:

> Now the essence of the greatest emotional appeal of bullfighting is the feeling of immortality that the bullfighter feels in the middle of a great faena and that he gives to the spectators. He is performing a work of art and he is playing with death, bringing it closer, closer, closer, to himself, a death that you know is in the horns because you have the canvas-covered bodies of the horses on the sand to prove it. He gives the feeling of his immortality, and, as you watch it, it becomes yours. Then when it belongs to both of you, he proves it with the sword.

The other, seven pages earlier, an astonishing sentence of 171 words, sums up Hemingway's point so well as to make much of the rest repetitious:

> If the spectators know the matador is capable of executing a complete, consecutive series of passes with the muleta in which there will be valor, art, understanding and, above all, beauty and great emotion, they will put up with mediocre work, cowardly work, disastrous work because they have the hope sooner or later of seeing the complete faena; the faena that takes a man out of himself and makes him feel immortal while it is proceeding, that gives him an ecstasy, that is, while momentary, as profound as any religious ecstasy; moving all the people in the ring together and increasing in emotional intensity as it proceeds, carrying the bullfighter with it, he playing on the crowd through the bull and being moved as it responds in a growing ecstasy of ordered, formal, passionate, increasing disregard for death that leaves you, when it is over, and the death administered to the animal that has made it possible, as empty, as changed and as sad as any major emotion will leave you.

80

Yes. There were a few things to say, practical or not. There are also Hemingway's now famous literary comments—allied with the bullfighter's dangerous purity of line—about clear statement as opposed to fakery, about connecting emotions with actions, about compression, about truth. Perhaps most illuminating is Hemingway's famous statement in this book that the writer may omit what he knows (a statement that a little compression and punctuation would have clarified):

> If a writer of prose knows enough about what he is writing about he may omit things that he knows and the reader, if the writer is writing truly enough, will have a feeling of those things as strongly as though the writer had stated them. The dignity of movement of an ice-berg is due to only one-eighth of it being above water. A writer who omits things because he does not know them only makes hollow places in his writing.

Or, as he was to say years later to Plimpton: "Anything you know you can eliminate and it only strengthens your iceberg." Perhaps the very trouble with *Death in the Afternoon* is that it tries to include rather than to eliminate: "If I could have made this enough of a book it would have had everything in it." And so, Hemingway produces a rococo monument, well out of water, rather than any dorsal fin of ice.

Hemingway's art is that of understatement, of suggestive silences. He learned the sights, sounds, smells, and sensations of Kid Howard's gym only to omit them in the end. His stories are not filled with these things; all is trimmed away but the occasional touch and the general word that goes home, that brings the collusive response. The central word in the iceberg statement is *feeling;* and *Death in the Afternoon* makes clear the emotive nature of Hemingway's work, so seemingly unemotional. In the soft, autobiographical Hemingway, his early best—"In Another Country," "Now I Lay Me," *The Sun Also Rises, A Farewell to Arms*—the emotion so bathes everything that the merest detail, warm chestnuts in the pocket, a bat flying about the room, touches the chord. In the hard Hemingway of "The Undefeated," we get the selected "actual things" that make the tragic emotion at the end.

For all its defects, *Death in the Afternoon* focuses Hemingway's interest in death as the universal antagonist, which each must eventually face alone. "It must be most dangerous then to be a man," says Hemingway's old lady (as he instructs her in venereal diseases). "It is indeed, madame," he replies, "and but few survive it. 'Tis a hard trade and the grave is at the end of it." There can be no happy endings: "There is no lonelier man in death, except the suicide, than that man who has lived many years with a good wife and then outlived her"—and his "Clean, Well-Lighted Place" was soon to illustrate the point. Death and its lonely confrontation haunted and fascinated Hemingway, and the fascination doubtless helped him repeatedly to test his courage in imagination and in fact against what he most dreaded. The bullfight and the big hunt allowed him to see the lonely test aesthetically and ritualistically—vicariously though with great intensity:

> When, lacking the technique and thereby admitting his inability to control his feet, the matador went down on both knees before the bull the crowd had no more sympathy with him than with a suicide.
>
> For myself, not being a bullfighter, and being much interested in suicides, the problem was one of depiction and waking in the night I tried to remember what it was that seemed just out of my remembering and that was the thing that I had really seen and, finally, remembering all around it, I got it. When he stood up, his face white and dirty and the silk of his breeches opened from waist to knee, it was the dirtiness of the rented breeches, the dirtiness of his slit underwear and the clean, clean, unbearably clean whiteness of the thigh bone that I had seen, and it was that which was important.

Although the good faenas gave him momentary sensations of immortality, they also emphasized the death toward which the moments carried him, along with the dead bullfighters, the dead animals:

> The great thing is to last and get your work done and see and hear and learn and understand; and write when there is something that you know; and not before; and not too damned much after. Let those who want to [,] save the world [—] if you can get to see it clear and as a whole. Then any part you make will represent the whole if it's made truly. The thing to do is work and learn to make it.

The true segment indeed suggests the true whole, though representation may be vastly incomplete. The authentic people, the authentic moments, do suggest an essential fact, which moves Hemingway in his final chapter and which he was to find again in Africa: life's transience makes life—any of it and all of it—vivid and vital and valuable. He would seem to be emphasizing, in Vergil's phrase, the tears of *things*. And in his last chapter the things stream by, once again through the mind and into the past. Four years later, when the Spanish Civil War finally boiled over, Hemingway found that

ERNEST HEMINGWAY AND ORDONEZ IN SPAIN, 1959

the Spain he had learned to love by following the ritual of death had moved him even to join those who wanted to save the world. The impressions recorded at the end of *Death in the Afternoon,* as Carlos Baker notes, well up again into *For Whom the Bell Tolls,* and the undefeated loser, first seen as a bullfighter who dies only for courage and the craft, becomes the man who will die for humanity.

✌ ☞

Winner Take Nothing, published October 27, 1933, a year after *Death in the Afternoon,* continues the impression that Hemingway is running down, and indicates that he had moved closer to the edge of despair. The book's epigraph is a piece of faked antiquity, printed between quotation marks:

> "Unlike all other forms of lutte or combat the conditions are that the winner shall take nothing; neither his ease, nor his pleasure, nor any notions of glory; nor, if he win far enough, shall there be any reward within himself."

Hemingway, still falling defensively into parody, wrote the epigraph himself, as he admitted to Carlos Baker in 1951. He then took his title from it. Life is single combat of a kind more hopeless than any chivalric society or writer could have imagined. Hemingway's undefeated loser has vanished, temporarily. Hemingway now imagines some dire test of arms that, if pushed far enough, will erase even the satisfaction of victory. The winner's prize is an inner emptiness, a Nothing, a Nada. Hemingway has concocted evidence to convince himself that the world is as bleak as his inner void at the time whispered it was.

The seven stories published in advance of the book indicate a reaching for new subjects and methods, and a growing depression. "Wine of Wyoming" (in *Scribner's Magazine,* August, 1930), the first story since 1927, the first after *A Farewell to Arms,* has little to recommend it beyond the curiosity of American prohibition in rural form, and the fact that it seems to be almost straight Hemingway autobiography. "The Sea Change" (*This Quarter,* Paris, December, 1931) tells of a man left by a lesbian mistress. "After the Storm" (*Cosmopolitan,* May, 1932—Hemingway's first publication on slick paper) is an eerie view of a sunken liner by a modern buccaneer, a man with glimmers of undefeat who will become Harry Morgan.

In the four stories of 1933 published in advance of the book, Hemingway's despair darkens. In "God Rest You Merry, Gentlemen," printed in 300 limited copies by a small publisher, Christian society has become a free turkey dinner in a saloon and moral suicide: a sixteen-year-old curly-haired boy, who has prayed night and day against sexual lust, cuts off his penis on Christmas and will surely die from loss of blood. The "I" of the story (not the amputee) is a young reporter covering the hospital beat in Kansas City who dreams of foreign lands, and who is teased for his name of "Horace"—Hemingway abusing himself again. "Homage to Switzerland" is a trivial experiment with form that nevertheless condemns American society with a final note of suicide. In three parallel stories, three Americans wait for the same train at the same time in three different Swiss stations along the line, simultaneously saying much the same things to identical waitresses in identical waiting rooms. Mr. Wheeler—notice the scorn in the "Mr."—is a homosexual; Mr. Johnson is a writer, miserable at thirty-five (Hemingway is now almost thirty-four) because his wife is divorcing him for another man, as is the American custom; Mr. Harris, whose initials are "E. H." and who has been living in Paris, discloses that his father has shot himself the year before:

> "I am truly sorry [says the aged lover of *The National Geographic* to whom he is talking]. I am sure his loss was a blow to science as well as to his family.
> "Science took it awfully well."

"Give Us a Prescription, Doctor," in the same issue of *Scribner's* (April, 1933) and renamed "The Gambler, the Nun, and the Radio," shows Hemingway's depression even more clearly. It is the better story, with a nun who loves the bad ones and prays in the chapel all Saturday afternoon that Notre Dame will win, and with a cheerful little Mexican gambler, silent against his pain in consideration for his wardmates, undaunted by a paralyzed leg. He has no luck, but believes that he might have, if he can just hold out long enough. (His name is Cayetano, as was Niño de la Palma's who went into *The Sun Also Rises*, remembered at the end of *Death in the Afternoon* as giving the bull's ear to Hadley—whose divorce has just been written into the preceding story.) Cayetano is another of the undefeated, but he merely underlines the misery of the middle-aged Nick at the center of the stage, now named "Mr. Frazer."

Mr. Frazer is a writer, derived, of course, from Hemingway himself, recuperating from his automobile crash. He knows that the nun and Our Lady would not like his work. He cries for an hour or so each night in his private room to relieve the pain in his leg, broken in a fall from a horse. He speaks Spanish to Cayetano, the lingua franca of the "bad ones," the inside-outsiders from whom he is as thoroughly alienated as was Nick within his group of Italian officers. He has "been through all this before," and his nerves have "become tricky." Socially conscious of the Marxist thirties, Mr. Frazer knows that liberty, "what we believed in," is "now the name of a MacFadden publication" (i.e., *Liberty Magazine*), and that religion, patriotism, economics, music, gambling, sexual intercourse, ambition, and the radio are all opiums of the people and all equally fallacious. The bootlegger who has furnished him the phrase has had a homosexual shock as an acolyte and now believes "in nothing." But drink, thinks Mr. Frazer, is "the sovereign opium of the people," and actually, in "that well-lighted part of his mind," where he finds himself thinking a little too well, he knows that bread is "the real, the actual opium of the people." Life itself, the daily bread, in other words, is a narcotic that keeps one from the awful truth. Give us a prescription, Doctor! As the little revolutionary guitarists and bootleggers leave, Frazer plans to "have a little spot of the giant killer" and to play the radio "so that you could hardly hear it," through another sleepless night.

"A Clean, Well-Lighted Place," published in the next issue of *Scribner's Magazine* (March, 1933), pushes Frazer's religious despair to a bottomless Nothing, "Nada," the "Nothing," eventually, of the book's title. Hemingway has recalled the word he had first applied to the religious procession in Pamplona: " 'Nada,' some one said. 'It's nothing. Drink up. Lift the bottle.' " The well-lighted part of Frazer's mind has become a clean, well-lighted café in Spain. The *nada* that was at first a mere happy indifference and then became a negative belief (with the disillusioned guitarist) is now the very bottom of nihilistic despair: "It was all a nothing and a man was nothing too." Even Frazer's bread, the people's opiate, comes squarely into the sacrilegious negation: "Our nada who art in nada. . . . Give us this nada our daily nada. . . . Hail nothing full of nothing, nothing is with thee."

The lonely waiter smiles at his desperate joke, a good deal farther into the night than Nick, his sleepless forerunner, who could still say his "Hail Marys," though in "Our Father" he had difficulty in getting beyond "on earth." Only drink and a clean, well-lighted place, where one may sit in the shadows of leaves, can sustain man from one black nothing to the next. The giant that Frazer's bottle kills is Nada. The deaf old man, who needs this sovereign opiate each night because he is "in despair," though he has plenty of money, cannot even hang himself: his niece has cut him down in fear for his soul. The despair of the story is indeed deeply touched with sympathy. The waiter wants to keep the café open less for himself than for anyone who, like him, might need a clean, light place in the night. His "nada" is sleepy and sad. After all, he says to himself, "it is probably only insomnia. Many must have it."

The story is classic Hemingway, much expressed with little showing, whittled and worthy of MacLeish, to whom Hemingway dedicates the book that contains it. He has compressed his dialogue so far, indeed, omitting identifying tags as never before, that he loses track of which waiter is saying what. Professor Otto Reinert has argued valiantly to explain away an error long since noticed by many readers and reported by Professors Colburn and Kroeger in *College English.* But his argument will not hold—that Hemingway the craftsman would not slip, that Hemingway here does twice what he does only rarely, and then by apparent accident—that is, he assigns two successive lines of dialogue to the same speaker.[1] We have, it appears, another symptom of a slippage evident in *Death in the Afternoon,* in *Winner Take Nothing* in general, and in the desperate nihilism of this particular story.

Flawed though it is, it strongly and sadly conveys that dryness of soul lurking in us all. A soldier and his girl go by, but the guard will pick him up. The young waiter's wife is waiting in bed for him, but the deaf old man has long ago lost his wife. He and the older waiter, who never had confidence, who cannot sleep without a light, know that, though some can live in it and never feel it, the black nada is always there. "There is no lonelier man in death, except the suicide, than that man who has lived many years with a good wife and then outlived her."

Winner Take Nothing, then, shows a certain unraveling of a superior talent. Six new stories join the seven already mentioned, to which Hemingway adds "A Natural History of the Dead," an instructive though tricked piece of journalism, now called a story, that had already appeared as part of *Death in the Afternoon,* as Hemingway, with strained humor, tells us in a footnote. Hemingway, the ex-journalist, again makes no distinction between a story and a news story.

The autobiographical content of *Winner Take Nothing* is high,

[1] See *To Have and Have Not,* pages 109, 134, written in haste; and *Across the River,* page 121.

and little heightened. The three Nick stories—"The Light of the World," "A Way You'll Never Be," "Fathers and Sons"—bracket the book as before, concluding the skeletal novel of Nick and repeating its structure. They brighten the book a little. The suicide of the father in "Homage to Switzerland" becomes the unspecified death and affectionate memory of the father in "Fathers and Sons," with which we conclude. The bloody and black anti-Christianity of "God Rest You Merry" and the "Well-Lighted Place" are balanced by the tigerish prizefighting son—"His own father shot and killed him"—who is the light of the world. But the remaining stories are, like the book generally, scattered and drab. "A Day's Wait," another father-and-son story, another about the fear of death, seems almost straight journalism. "The Mother of the Queen" is about a homosexual bullfighter; "One Reader Writes" is a lovelorn letter from a wife whose husband has "sifilus."

6

✑ GREEN HILLS AND THE GULF

EIGHT of the fourteen stories in *Winner Take Nothing* are set
in America, and a ninth, "Homage to Switzerland," makes clear
that for Hemingway America represented some lost innocence. But
he continued to fish in American waters. In September, 1933, in
Madrid, he had written "One Trip Across," developing the saga of
Harry Morgan from "After the Storm." At the same time, *Esquire*
(Autumn, 1933) published "Marlin off the Morro," a factual account from the Gulf Stream, which began Hemingway's three solid
years with the American prince of slicks. Hemingway was working off his Nada. He was making money. He was soon to discover
Africa, as a means of exploring America and himself.

In 1922, Hemingway had first responded to Africa in reviewing
René Maran's *Batouala*. In 1930, hunting in Wyoming, he had
written to Perkins that he was "still" dreaming of Africa. By 1932,
he had read Mungo Park's eighteenth-century *Travels in the Interior
Districts of Africa*. In November, 1933, he and Mrs. Hemingway
sailed from Marseille, having been abroad, from Key West, since
August. By mid-December, their automotive safari, with Charles
Thompson of Key West and Philip Percival, their professional
British hunter, was camped in British East Africa. In January,
1934, amoebic dysentery sent Hemingway by one-passenger plane
past Mount Kilimanjaro to Nairobi. He rejoined the party for a
final month of hunting, before the rains would send them toward
the coast on February 18. He began *Green Hills of Africa* on his
return to Key West in early April, 1934, and had it cut and pol-
ished by February 7, 1935. *Scribner's Magazine* serialized it from
May to October, and Scribner's published the book on October 25,
1935.

The flow of articles in *Esquire* had continued, nine in twelve issues in 1934, twelve in twelve in 1935. Hemingway's fifteenth
consecutive issue (February, 1936) printed "The Tradesman's Re-

turn," Hemingway's first story in two years, picking up Harry Morgan in what was to become Part II of *To Have and Have Not*. The June *Esquire*, after two more reports from the Gulf, printed "The Horns of the Bull" (renamed "The Capital of the World" for *The Fifth Column*), Hemingway's last bullfighting story and a beautifully ironic demonstration, as Edmund Wilson pointed out, of a boy's illusions and the world's tarnished realities. In August, 1936, *Esquire* published "The Snows of Kilimanjaro," the last of the Hemingway run (except for three minor pieces more than two years later). In September, *Cosmopolitan* published "The Short Happy Life of Francis Macomber," which Hemingway was to choose for *This Is My Best* (edited by Whit Burnett, 1942), though he later thought that, of his stories, "The Snows" was "about as good as any."

Green Hills of Africa, almost universally put down as "unsatisfactory" by judges of Hemingway's fiction, is actually Hemingway's most mature book, a pleasure and a surprise after darkest Nada. Simply as an account of big-game hunting, it is excellent. In his final month of hunting, Hemingway saw a natural anecdote of success and failure. To give the anecdote point, he sets it, in a long retrospective detour, against the trip's earlier triumphs and frustrations. At every turn he has come in second. He shoots a lion his wife missed, only to have the boys carry his wife into camp in triumph. He gets a rhinoceros, only to find his friend already in camp with a bigger one. A truck spoils his chance for kudu. Time grows shorter. Then, alone in new hunting grounds, on the last day, just at dusk, he miraculously kills two kudu with one shot each. Back to camp, jubilant, he finds his friend with a bigger one. But he and the reader will have the memory:

> I looked at him, big, long-legged, a smooth gray with the white stripes and the great, curling, sweeping horns, brown as walnut meats, and ivory pointed, at the big ears and the great, lovely heavy-maned neck the white chevron between his eyes and the white of his muzzle and I stooped over and touched him to try to believe it. He was lying on the side where the bullet had gone in and there was not a mark on him and he smelled sweet and lovely like the breath of cattle and the odor of thyme after rain.

Hemingway has worked from "the shape of a country and the pattern of a month's action." Dusty plains, with mud-red rhinoceroses and reeking baboons, contrast with green hills and sweet kudu, as Carlos Baker says. And the natural pattern of pursuit contains it all, beautifully told, and beautifully illustrated in pen and ink by Edward Shenton.

The story of personal failure is a personal triumph. The four sections—"Pursuit and Conversation," "Pursuit Remembered," "Pursuit and Failure," "Pursuit as Happiness"—suggest that pursuit is better than victory, and that Hemingway is pursuing more than animals. He is hunting truth and a way of life, in a new confrontation of language and self, in the old struggle with journalism and literature: "The writer has attempted to write an absolutely true book to see whether the shape of a country and the pattern of a month's action can, if truly presented, compete with a work of the imagination." An absolutely true book versus a work of the imagination! Have his previous works of the imagination seemed *untrue?* "Tell him I'm ashamed of being a writer," says Bill Gorton to the bullfighter, the man of action, in *The Sun Also Rises.* The writer in "Homage to Switzerland" feels much the same way. In Africa, Hemingway faced the facts and himself, still not ready to believe what he might have learned from Fielding, and what finally, in his fifty-ninth year, he knew, when Plimpton asked him, "Why a representation of fact, rather than fact itself?" Hemingway replied,

> Why be puzzled by that? From things that have happened and from things as they exist and from all things that you know and all those you cannot know, you make something through your invention that is not a representation but a whole new thing truer than anything true and alive, and you make it alive, and if you make it well enough, you give it immortality.

In *Green Hills,* Hemingway was on the way to this healing belief. In *Death in the Afternoon* he had not yet made a clear distinction between fact and fiction. *Green Hills* stabilized him, though fiction for him was still oddly different from truth, as a remark to Plimpton shows: "The Snows of Kilimanjaro" and "The Short Happy Life of Francis Macomber" are "stories which I invented from the knowledge and experience acquired on the same long hunting trip one month of which I had tried to write a *truthful* [my italics] account of in the *Green Hills.*"

In this truthful account, Hemingway is facing himself for the first time, admitting, bravely, that he has a wife, that he is jealous, boastful, unreasonable, sulking. Stronger each day after his dysentery, he is doing what he likes and knowing that somehow it is right, though beyond his powers of explanation. He is happy, and knows his defects:

> Oh, yes. He writes [says Mrs. Hemingway]. When he's going well he's awfully easy to get along with. But just before he gets going he's frightful. His temper has to go bad before he can write. When he talks about never writing again I know he's about to get started.

And as she and Pop continue to tease Hemingway about being a writer, tracker, and wing shot, we know that Hemingway has been through the Nada.

The new confidence is everywhere. The prose is free of *Death in the Afternoon,* of self-consciousness, newly intricate and at ease (at least, so it seems to me; Young finds the book full of posturing). Hemingway's new touch of British seems right ("feel a fool," "bloody"), since he in fact and in prose is emulating the excellent Pop, the British hunter. Figures of speech pruned from his earlier work and bandied in embarrassment by the tauromaniac are now the natural expressions of a man trying to pin down what he sees, what he feels, what he thinks: "that electric speed that meant that he was racing the little nickelled death inside him"—locusts making the sky "seem a pink dither of flickering passage, flickering like an old cinema film, but pink instead of gray"—"the smell of the regiment like a copper coin in your mouth."

The truck that spoils his evening kudu, as the book opens, carries an Austrian in Tyrolean pants who remembers Hemingway from the early *Querschnitt*: "The *dichter*. You know Hemingway the poet?" Hemingway is pleased. "The Undefeated," and perhaps the poems —since *dichter* and *poet* could mean simply *writer* to the Austrian— have made their mark. This leads to a famous interview on American literature, about which Plimpton later asked:

> Do you think a writer's power diminishes as he grows older? In the *Green Hills of Africa* you mention that American writers at a certain age change into Old Mother Hubbards. HEMINGWAY: I don't know about that. People who know what they are doing should last as long [as] their heads last. In that book you mention, if you look it up, you'll see I was sounding off about American literature with a humorless Austrian character who was forcing me to talk when I wanted to do something else. I wrote an accurate account of the conversation. Not to make deathless pronouncements. A fair per cent of the pronouncements are good enough.

This conversation, apparently irrelevant, nevertheless gives Africa an American reference that runs throughout the book, stirring Hemingway's thoughts—as he cools his boots outside the truck or cools his heels in the dust of a blind—with the question of writing, of America, of himself as American writer, and of his own life against the American background. First, he is sure that his writing is worth doing in itself. With discipline, with an "absolue conscience as unchanging as the standard meter in Paris, to prevent faking," with intelligence, disinterestedness, and the luck to survive, he knows that one can reach a fourth and fifth dimension, a prose never yet written, more difficult to achieve than poetry. This is the ideal, and he means to strive for it. He knows that, for him, writing and the enjoyment of his life are cognate. He feels that modern America ruins its writers with money and ambition, that early America ruined them with gentility, salvation, and rhetoric. "They did not use the words that people always have used in speech, the words that survive in language."

Hemingway, as Robert Penn Warren has said, is very close to Wordsworth in his drive to get back to simple language and simple people. And we realize from his African rumination that he is indeed close to that great and peculiar American Romantic he mentions next: Henry David Thoreau, whom he cannot yet read, but hopes to read later. "I cannot read *other* [my italics] naturalists unless they are being extremely accurate and not literary." Hemingway, then, is a naturalist. He is looking for truth through nature. No transcendentalist, no philosopher, surely, he nevertheless departs America only to think about it, and to get himself into perspective. Africa is his Walden Pond, though Hemingway himself would have scoffed at the notion.

In what may be a paraphrase of Thoreau (for Hemingway had obviously tried to read him), Hemingway speaks of wanting to come again to Africa really to live: "Not just let my life pass." Like Thoreau, who said that a boy with a gun would eventually revere nature and leave the gun behind, Hemingway the hunter says:

> I'd see the buffalo feeding where they lived, and when the elephants came through the hills we could see them and watch them breaking branches and not have to shoot, and I would lie in the fallen leaves and watch the kudu feed out and never fire a shot unless I saw a better head than this one in back, and instead of trailing that sable bull, gut-shot to hell, all day, I'd lie behind a rock and watch them on the hillside and see them long enough so they belonged to me forever.

Ernest Hemingway

Like a lustier Thoreau, Hemingway comes, through nature, or "country," to a validity of feeling that moves him beyond the flow of time. The meaning of life is in his mind itself, the clear moments against the flow, the sweetness of a Now that passes even as it comes. He wants to get back to an Africa he has not yet left, as, awake in the night, he "would lie, listening, homesick for it already":

> Now, looking out the tunnel of trees over the ravine at the sky with white clouds moving across in the wind, I loved the country so that I was happy as you are after you have been with a woman that you really love, when, empty, you feel it welling up again and there it is and you can never have it all and yet what there is, now, you can have, and you want more and more, to have, and be, and live in, to possess now again for always, for that long, sudden-ended always; making time stand still, sometimes so very still that afterwards you wait to hear it move, and it is slow in starting.

The book is really a beautiful self-justification, as Thoreau's is, for rejecting society so that life can be lived in the only place a man can live it: in himself. From the first, with no clear intention, Hemingway had rebelled against American society, setting himself to work out his way alone. Africa brings him close to an understanding of what he has done. He has turned away from an American literature that seems false and an American society that seems either a stock exchange or (under the National Recovery Act of the depressed thirties) a brotherhood of dependence: "Some sort of Y. M. C. A. show. Starry eyed bastards spending money that somebody will have to pay. Everybody in our town quit work to go on relief. Fishermen all turned carpenters. Reverse of the Bible."

America, in Hemingway's eyes, is finished, the frontier gone; but in rejecting it he is being typically American: "Our people went to America because that was the place to go then. It had been a good country and we had made a bloody mess of it and I would go, now, somewhere else . . . as we had always gone." Africa and the hunt, and the writing and perceiving of it, become Hemingway's Declaration of Independence, on which he puns (as Carlos Baker has said) for the title of his last section: "Pursuit as Happiness." Hemingway has a cruder form of Thoreau's completely American instinct to discover what a man is like alone in a wilderness not too far from town.

And even while greenest Africa looms ahead as God's country, Hemingway thinks of it in terms of Michigan and the American Gulf: "I loved this country and I felt at home and where a man feels at home, outside of where he's born, is where he's meant to go. Then, in my grandfather's time, Michigan was a malaria ridden state. . . ." In the midst of wild Africa, his supreme symbol of the wilderness of experience and the flow of time is those blue American waters just off Cuba, in which he will find his last and finest book: "this Gulf Stream you are living with, knowing, learning about, and loving, has moved, as it moves, since before man . . . and the palm fronds of our victories, the worn light bulbs of our discoveries and the empty condoms of our great loves float with no significance against one single, lasting thing—the stream." "So, in the front seat, thinking of the sea and the country," Hemingway's meditation runs, in a glorious four-hundred-word sentence, almost to metaphysics, as far as it will ever go, musing over the green hills, or over a page of Tolstoy, in the midday heat, at the edge of a rhinoceros marsh.

The mystery of literature comes home. He lives in the Russian forest as the wind rustles Africa overhead. He thinks of how Tolstoy's Russia and Stendahl's France were as immediate to them as the Michigan of his boyhood or the walk across Milan to the Ospidale Maggiore were to him. The transience and permanence of experience are again in his mind, as at the end of *Death in the Afternoon.* Memories drift in italics, as they will soon do in "The Snows of Kilimanjaro." The mystery of consciousness and the power of literature revolve through the pleasant heat: "For we have been there in the books and out of the books—and where we go, if we are any good, there you can go as we have been."

Hemingway's new honesty of self reaches a new selflessness. He can at last record his angers and self-righteous quarrels—"He's not a damned show-off like me." All the old theatrics are absorbed in the new maturity, except for the slight relapse of the Foreword, still slightly torrential and Fieldingesque: "Any one not finding sufficient love interest is at liberty, while reading it, to insert whatever love interest he or she may have at the time." Actually, Hemingway's love for his wife and his deep affection for Pop are wholly sufficient and interesting, a pleasant triangle, on the subsoil of which Macomber's short happiness is to be built:

I was looking at P. O. M., very desirable, cool, and neat-looking in her khaki and her boots, her Stetson on one side of her head, and at

Pop, big, thick, in the faded corduroy sleeveless jacket that was almost white now from washing and the sun.

And again:

Her courage was so automatic and so much a simple state of being that she never thought of danger; then, too, danger was in the hands of Pop and for Pop she had a complete, clear-seeing, absolutely trusting adoration. Pop was her ideal of how a man should be, brave, gentle, comic, never losing his temper, never bragging, never complaining except in a joke, tolerant, understanding, intelligent. drinking a little too much as a good man should, and, to her eyes, very handsome.

Hemingway and his wife and Pop are as solid and attractive as anyone Hemingway ever put on paper; and we like Hemingway in spite of his faults in the way Pop likes him, or in the way of old M'Cola, distrusting at first, admiring at last, plucking a leaf to shave the sweat from his pate as he teases Hemingway about his whisky.

The beauty of the book gathers at the end: this is not simply a book about Africa, nor about America, nor about the mystery of writing and being; it is also a tribute to a man and a woman loved:

"You know," P. O. M. said, "I can't remember it. I can't remember Mr. J. P.'s face. And he's beautiful. I think about him and think about him and I can't see him. It's terrible. He isn't the way he looks in a photograph. In a little while I won't be able to remember him at all. Already I can't see him."

"You must remember him," Karl said to her.

"I can remember him," I said. "I'll write you a piece some time and put him in."

Hemingway has done it, too: the portrait of Pop, written for her. And the truth of the friendship, the truth that friendships part, moves us in a way one would have thought beyond the reach of the tough romantic.

༈ ༈

But the irritations just barely shadowing the green hills immediately produced two of Hemingway's best stories, the last ones of any significance. Hemingway's dysentery and his flight past Kilimanjaro triggered the first, and in both we can almost see events transpose themselves from *Green Hills* into fiction, as Young already sug-

96

gested. Both stories illustrate the failing America Hemingway has
mentioned. In both, as in *Green Hills,* an able Englishman represents human excellence. In both, Hemingway dramatizes his buried
antagonisms against the wife he loves, and whom four years later
he divorced. The inner meditations on life and writing become "The
Snows of Kilimanjaro." The outer triangulation of Hemingway,
P. O. M., and Pop becomes "The Short Happy Life of Francis Macomber."

In "The Snows," Harry, a writer, and his rich wife are camped,
waiting for a plane to fly Harry to a hospital. He has "come out
here to start again"—to Africa, "where he had been happiest in the
good time of his life." Hemingway is projecting his wished-for
return into his feared decay and death. Harry has scratched his
knee while trying to photograph a herd of waterbuck (Hemingway
the new naturalist with the old damaged knee). Gangrene has set
in. Vultures squat, and a hyena slinks at the edge of the odor.
Harry has sold his talent for sex and wealth, illustrating Hemingway's remark in *Green Hills* that "politics, women, drink, money,
and ambition" damage American writers. As Philip Young says,
the wealthy Mrs. Hemingway, and the easy Key West life, are certainly in the picture, though touches from the F. Scott Fitzgeralds
may also be evident, as Carlos Baker suggests.

But the honest marital bickering of *Green Hills* turns vicious—
"trying to kill to keep yourself alive"—as the same Molo from the
real trip brings whisky and soda, as before. Harry, dying, thinks
of what he would have written if he had not gone soft, if he had
only had time. But unlike the similar italicized memories in *Green
Hills,* in which we can see details that had already gone into Nick
Adams and Frederic Henry, the dying writer thinks mostly of things
that Hemingway, in fact, had not written about. Hemingway, in
other words, who several times has mentioned stories "known" but
not yet written, is drawing intimately on the writer's fears that he
should cease to be. Since his first sketch of dying Maera, Hemingway had not tried to portray the event that haunted him. This
portrayal is far more moving, and is probably as complete as anyone, short of clairvoyance, can make it, as life yearns itself onward
even at its end.

The story's main spring is a universal self-pity, that which produces the frequent childhood fantasy of one's own death, pale
among the lilies, appreciated too late. Harry is punishing his wife,
who does not fully believe him dying, until, heart pounding, she
sees him dead. But the ultimate spell of the story, in addition to

its authenticity and its crisp reminder of time's transience, comes from Hemingway's new figurative symbolism—a leopard borrowed from Dante and a mountain from Flaubert, as Alfred G. Angstrom has shown. For the first time in his fiction, Hemingway is using metaphor to render states of feeling. Death comes "with a rush; not as a rush of water nor of wind; but of a sudden evil-smelling emptiness and the odd thing was that the hyena slipped lightly along the edge of it." And the metaphor moves into a calculated symbolism different from that in the earlier Hemingway where actual rivers, and fish, and chestnuts take on a symbolic shadow from the feeling attached to them. The hyena is actual, to be sure, but Hemingway makes him a progressive symbol of death, recurrent in a way not found earlier.

Harry, speechless, with death crouched on his chest, is next aware that it is morning. The plane comes with the competent British Compton. Then below he sees a cloud of locusts, now not a "pink dither" but white like the first winter blizzard. Then they head for the white top of Kilimanjaro, and Harry knows that that is where he is going.

"Just then the hyena stopped whimpering in the night and started to make a strange, human, almost crying sound." Hemingway completes the eerie transmigration of Harry's soul by putting an epigraph at the head of his story. The Masai call the western summit of Kilimanjaro "The House of God," he says; and near it is "the dried and frozen carcass of a leopard. No one has explained what the leopard was seeking at that altitude." Harry, apparently, is frozen eternally short of God in spite of his seeking. But, as Young points out, Harry has reached a kind of perfection after all, the gangrenous flesh exchanged for eternally preserved leopard, suggesting the writer's wish for immortal work, also expressed in *Green Hills*.

~§ §~

Francis Macomber, like Harry, has come to Africa to find himself, and grows to manhood under fire a few moments before his violent death. "Murder," the critics continue to assume—in the teeth of Hemingway's statement: "Mrs. Macomber, in the car, had shot at the buffalo with the 6.5 Mannlicher as it seemed about to gore Macomber and had hit her husband about two inches up and a little to one side of the base of his skull." Clearly, it is an accident. Margot Macomber has seen her husband bolt in a lion hunt. She has visited their British hunter's cot. Macomber and Wilson have knocked down three buffalo, after an illegal chase by car, with Macomber shooting well, partly from anger, partly because he hasn't had time to think. Margot loses her American female dominance as her husband comes of age before her eyes. She slowly goes to pieces in the corner of the car, "very afraid of something."

When Macomber stands up to the charging bull but fails to stop him, Margot instinctively attempts to save him and thus put him back in his place. But she is no hunter, and Macomber's new masculinity has left her shaken. She shoots at the buffalo but kills her husband, in a beautiful ironic twist. Attempting to save the day and save her dominance, she immortalizes the bravery that has defeated her. Wilson, who knows it was an accident, completes her annihilation by implying, momentarily, that she shot her husband to keep him from leaving her: "He would have left you too"— "Why didn't you poison him? That's what they do in England." The American woman is worse than poison. She has "had something on him": chasing by car would have cost him his license and put him out of business. Now he has something on her to keep her quiet.

As in *Green Hills* and "The Snows," Africa and its British stand as indictments of American society. Wilson lives by "good form." Bravery is no problem: one simply does what a man ought. Wilson is the prime exhibit of Hemingway's "Code Hero," a man less frequent and complete in Hemingway than the label suggests—a label that has nicely confused the issue as to who is hero and what is code. America has lost the bravery Wilson personifies. The glittering American female has softened the men into boys, or picked them soft. But it does not matter when you die but how well, like the dying lion, recast from Hemingway's thoughts in *Green Hills,* digging his claws in.

The story reaches visibly back through *Green Hills.* Wilson is a shorter, younger, redder Pop, with the same phrases, the same husky voice; and with Pop's fatherly affection turned to an admiring and hostile adultery. Margot Macomber has Mrs. Hemingway's wit, brightness, and dark hair. But she is enameled with malice, and takes her name from some beautiful Margot of the Hemingways' acquaintance, mentioned as they discuss Pop's pulchritude. And the very tall, crew-cut Macomber, athlete and sportsman, the all-American boy of thirty-five, has a great deal of Hemingway in him in spite of the Princeton physique. Their ages are almost identical: during his African trip Hemingway was six months short of his thirty-fifth birthday, and he wrote the story when he was thirty-six. Like Hemingway, Macomber is good with a Springfield. From British Wilson, Macomber hears the lines from *Henry IV* that Hemingway's admired British friend, Captain Eric Edward Dorman-Smith, of His Majesty's Fifth Fusiliers, had written out for him in Milan—lines that Hemingway took as "a permanent protecting talisman," as he says in his "Introduction" to *Men at War*: "a man can die but once; we owe God a death . . . he that dies this year is quit for the next." Hemingway has thought affectionately of Dorman-Smith, "old chink," toward the end of *Green Hills*: "Pop and chink were much alike."

Three experiences recorded in *Green Hills* become Macomber's. First is Mrs. Hemingway's false triumph over the lion, as Macomber is carried into camp on native shoulders for the lion that he had run from and Wilson had shot. "You know in Africa no woman ever misses her lion and no white man ever bolts," says Wilson, explaining that the customer is always right; but mention of "woman," irrelevant here, uncovers Hemingway's resentment over the lion he shot for his wife. Into the lion hunt also goes Hemingway's adventure into tall grass, with Mrs. Hemingway anxiously looking on, as Carlos Baker has noted. Macomber's three buffalo are Hemingway's three, with his distaste for "riding in cars" added:

> I was thinking of the buff the way I had seen them when we had gotten the three that time, how the old bull had come out of the bush, groggy as he was, and I could see the horns, the boss coming far down, the muzzle out, the little eyes, the roll of fat and muscle on his thin-haired, gray, scaly-hided neck, the heavy power and the rage in him, and I admired him and respected him, but he was slow, and all the while we shot I felt that it was fixed and that we had him.

But now Hemingway is going into tall grass after another wounded buffalo, thinking ahead about how he must "put it down his nose" (Wilson's phrase in the story), how he will try one last shot in the bullfighter's spot between the shoulders before he goes sideways into the grass. He is sure of himself, feeling the elation he is to give Macomber:

> Now, going forward, sure he was in there, I felt the elation, the best elation of all, of certain action to come, action in which you had something to do, in which you can kill and come out of it, doing something you are ignorant about and so not scared, no one to worry about and no responsibility except to perform something you feel sure you can perform. . . .

At this point, Mrs. Hemingway, not hearing whispered directions, comes up from behind with M'Cola, slightly unnerving the two hunters. Earlier she and M'Cola had come up from behind, M'Cola with the Springfield cocked for her protection, a violation of safety rules that infuriated Hemingway. This buffalo gets away, but we can see him again, surely, in the one that comes for Francis Macomber, whose well-intending wife kills him from behind, after he has, for the first time in his life, "really felt wholly without fear," experiencing instead "a feeling of definite elation," and speaking to Wilson about "a feeling of happiness at action to come." Hemingway, who liked to make the Swahili *m'uzuri* into sentences about Missouri and Arkansas, has also made himself as "Bwana M'Kumba" into "Francis Macomber" (M'Kumba seems to be Hemingway's transcription of *mkubwa*, "chief"), drawing another slightly effeminate portrait of what he did not like in himself, christening the irony in "Chief" an effeminate "Francis." And as he would wish for himself, Macomber grows up and goes down bravely, an undefeated loser. Young points out that Hemingway may also have adopted his story of precipitation into bravery under fire from Crane's *Red Badge of Courage,* a book later anthologized by Hemingway, and a writer praised in *Green Hills.*

Although Hemingway soldiers a little whenever he speaks of hunting as "an action," both "Macomber" and the book behind it show Hemingway at his best. In both he sights his subject steadily. The story compresses the social criticism and the self-justification of the book with a new and breathtaking sureness of understated psychology and plot. Indeed, it is Hemingway's only plotted short story outside the tough world of stories like "My Old Man," "Fifty Grand," and "One Trip Across."

By the middle of July, 1936, before his two African stories appeared in print, Hemingway had decided to extend "One Trip Across" and "The Tradesman's Return" into a book about "the decline of the individual," which was to become *To Have and Have Not.* In *Green Hills* he had already mentioned writing "a study" of revolutions, after what he had recently seen in Cuba. He had also seen rioting in Genoa in 1922, and the first Spanish revolution in 1931. His mind in Africa had turned westward: "The best sky was in Italy and Spain and Northern Michigan in the fall and in the fall in the Gulf off Cuba." The repeated "fall" is a curious echo from Joyce, whom he had just mentioned. Hemingway had also seen the Depression at work off Key West, particularly among the veterans building causeways along the Florida Keys under the Federal Emergency Reconstruction Act. He had written an account for *The New Masses* of 200 veterans drowned by hurricane through what seemed bureaucratic negligence. His African indictment of America was turning into the kind of social consciousness in which his contemporaries had found him lacking.

Between Cuba and Key West, between what revolution and depression do to different people, Hemingway planned to launch his buccaneer Harry Morgan, the last individual. The real Henry Morgan, whose treasure is perhaps still buried somewhere near those waters, will now be an ex-policeman, a chartered-boat fisherman, and a rumrunner, significantly called not "Henry" but "Harry"— a curious counterpart, as Carlos Baker remarks, of Harry, the writer decaying near Kilimanjaro. In Harry Morgan, Hemingway will blend something of his friend Captain Joe Russell of Key West with some of the glamour of Howard Pyle's *Book of Pirates*— though it mentions Morgan only once, in passing—which Hemingway had recently been reading to one of his sons, if we may take the data of "A Day's Wait" as factual.

But on July 17, 1936, just as Hemingway laid his plans for *To Have and Have Not,* the Spanish Civil War erupted. Hemingway ended his gentleman's agreement with *Esquire* and went to Montana to complete his book with a third Morgan story. He finished the first draft on January 2, 1937, enlarged to include a socially conscious Key West writer, a public success and private failure, the opposite of Harry Morgan. Hemingway sailed for Spain on February 27, as correspondent for the North American Newspaper Alliance, still dissatisfied with the enlargement. On May 19, he was back in New York to complete the script for *The Spanish Earth,* a film on which he collaborated with director Joris Ivens and photographer John Ferno. In June, he spoke before the Writer's Congress on behalf of the Loyalists. On July 8, Hemingway and Ivens showed their film to President and Mrs. Roosevelt at the White House. He had continued to doctor *To Have and Have Not,* reading and revising proof from July 18 until August 7.

On August 11, 1937, Hemingway tussled famously in Maxwell Perkins's office with his old friend Max Eastman. Hemingway had bared his bosom to refute Eastman's query, in a review entitled "Bull in the Afternoon," as to why Hemingway's writing seemed to wear false hair on its chest. The feud seems an old one. Hemingway had flared up at Eastman, as Loeb tells us, fifteen years before, in Paris. Now old Paris friends—including MacLeish, who was backing the anti-Fascist film with Hemingway—sprang to defend Hemingway's virility. No one to this day has reported, I think, that Eastman had merely appropriated Hemingway's own words about a bullfighter in the book Eastman was reviewing, *Death in the Afternoon*: "he laid his bravery on as with a trowel. It was as though he were constantly showing you the quantity of hair on his chest or the way he was built in his more private parts." On August 14, 1937, Hemingway sailed again for Spain. On October 15, Scribner's published the still unsatisfactory *To Have and Have Not*.

Even so, *To Have and Have Not* comes near to equaling Hemingway's best. Although social consciousness spoils it with pat affairs of the rich and a message on the hero's lips, the novel is Hemingway's first to create a hero. Jake Barnes, in his endurance, had come close; and so had Henry, in his active phase. Both had represented modern man incapable before chaos. But Harry Morgan is heroic, as Jack Brennan was heroic, made of the same undefeated ingenuity, and presented at length. Again a beautifully tough and limited character gives us an ironically delimited world. The style enriched on green hills is now colloquially salted:

> She watched him go out of the house, tall, wide-shouldered, flat-backed, his hips narrow, moving, still, she thought, like some kind of animal, easy and swift and not old yet, he moves so light and smooth-like, she thought. . . .

And once more:

> . . . then the rod bent double and the reel commenced to screech and out he came, boom, in a long straight jump, shining silver in the sun and making a splash like throwing a horse off a cliff.

Again, an amusing and pathetic view through a clear, simple mind:

> Just then the old man with the long gray hair over the back of his collar who sells the rubber goods specialties comes in for a quarter of a pint and Freddy pours it out for him and he corks it up and scuttles back across the street with it.

Hemingway's structure derives from his idiom, and with a new virtuosity, as it catches Morgan and society from different angles. Harry Morgan had told the first story in his own words. Hemingway had pushed the second story all the way into the third person: Morgan throughout is merely "the man." To unify the book Hemingway had to continue to vary the view, and he discovered a breadth of contrast that was to serve him again, and well, in *For Whom the Bell Tolls*. Admittedly, he loses control—Part III takes up two thirds of the book—but his gain is considerable. He seems to be reaching for the "fifth dimension," mentioned in *Green Hills* and developed in *For Whom the Bell Tolls*, as F. I. Carpenter has explained—a William Jamesian simultaneity of events that lifts us beyond our ordinary perceptions in time and space.

And for the first time in a novel, Hemingway uses plot. Each of his high-school stories had depended on plot. "My Old Man" had continued the line. But success with mood and a single predicament had set plot aside until "Fifty Grand" (1927), not to appear again until "One Trip Across" (1934) and "Macomber" (1936). The unique "Macomber" excepted, plot has risen in Hemingway's mind only from the shrewd world he had first attempted to draw in "A Matter of Color." With Harry Morgan as with Jack Brennan, necessity is the mother of invention, and invention displays the hero's enviable wits and courage. The plot itself, cryptic through understatement, challenges and wins our admiration in its three separate pulses. Starting with separate stories, Hemingway has had to align his events toward one end in a way so able that we wish the end had held, and that he had tried again.

The end is to show Morgan progressively beaten in spite of his splendid intentions and abilities. He is trying to support a wife and three daughters in Key West by chartering his boat for fishing off touristic Havana. Loss of his expensive fishing reel leads to loss of his hire and the end of his fishing. This in turn leads to carrying illegal Chinese, and then to a murder, which ends that possibility. Next he must try the unprofitable rumrunning of the post-Prohibition days. This leads to loss of his arm by gunfire. His crippled arm leads to his arrest, as he tries to bury his treasure of bootlegged liquor in shallow water. This leads to loss of his boat. Determined to make his own living and keep his family off relief, he makes the desperate contract with Cuban revolutionaries that kills him. Everything fits, including a high WPA truck that sights his hidden boat, and the loss of arm that hobbles his shooting.

But Morgan's dying words do not fit. Probable enough, moving enough, Morgan's death nevertheless gives us a message when we want a man. Instead of "a man alone has no chance," we want the old ironic, undefeated "I was really going good." We want the uselessness of Morgan's single-handed and single-minded integrity to illuminate its glory. We want another little bullfighter, in another sorry contest, beaten but undefeated.

The other Key West characters light up both the uselessness and the glory. All are getting along, one way or another, depression notwithstanding. Freddy Wallace, Morgan's coequal, owns a sparkling boat and a bar. Freddy is, in fact, as was Morgan in part, modeled from Hemingway's successful fishing friend, Russell. Even the battered veterans, whose Saturday night in Freddy's bar is a poetic rendition of one Hemingway witnessed in Russell's, are surviving. Harry's angry independence is his tragedy and his glory. Freddy, and Hayzoos ("Jesus") the cab driver, and even Eddy the rummy and Albert, are demonstrating that a man alone does have a chance. Hemingway did not clearly see this irony in his evidence. If he did, he would have achieved the final twist his story suggests. He would have let us know that Harry's dying words are painfully and ironically wrong, instead of presenting them as patently right, in a social message from the author, which everything in the story has worked against.

This is an error worse than that usually noted: that Hemingway loses Harry among sketches of high life on the Florida Keys, as indeed he does. Sentences would have sufficed for sections, and we could do without the cluster of Wallaces: a bouncer named Wallace works for Freddy (Wallace), and we soon run into the Wallace Johnston with whom we began, and who has an effeminate friend named Henry. Time would have cured much of this, and much is excellent: the monologue of the lonesome adulteress, contrasting with Morgan's last night with his wife and her final monologue; Mrs. Richard Gordon's angry epithet—"You writer"; Gordon's comeuppance at the bar, and his view of Marie Morgan.

This last, which Delmore Schwartz found the worst moment in a bad book, is actually one of Hemingway's subtlest effects. It is his fullest denunciation of the untruth of fiction, his sharpest caricature of the writer as eager illusionist and social microbe. It deepens the essential fineness of roughneck Harry, who worships his bedraggled wife as she worships him. We have their last night in mind; we have just left Harry dying. Then, in the next chapter, Richard Gordon on his bicycle passes "a heavy-set, big, blue-eyed woman, with bleached-blond hair showing under her old man's felt hat, hurrying across the road, her eyes red from crying." He gets home, snaps at his own wife, and starts to write:

> In today's chapter he was going to use the big woman with the tear-reddened eyes. . . . Her husband when he came home at night hated her, hated the way she had coarsened and grown heavy, was repelled by her bleached hair, her too big breasts, her lack of sympathy with

his work as an organizer. He would compare her to the young, firm-breasted, full-lipped little Jewess that had spoken at the meeting that evening. It was good. It was, it could be easily, terrific, and it was true. He had seen, in a flash of perception, the whole inner life of that type of woman.

At last the parodic spring torrents are working, ironically contrasting the false fictional world with the "true" world it misinterprets. The irony is completed when, in Marie's final reminiscence, we have young Harry breathless with adoration of the newly bleached hair.

Satire and comedy work with Hemingway's insistent despair to produce a genuine human being, in an expansion of that pathos touched in "The Undefeated" and "Fifty Grand," the tragic comedy of the limited view:

> He sat at the table and looked at the piano, the sideboard and the radio, the picture of September Morn, and the pictures of the cupids holding bows behind their heads, the shiny, real-oak table and the shiny real-oak chairs and the curtains on the windows and he thought, What chance have I to enjoy my home?

Or again, Harry's reiteration, on the night of his last crossing: "a nice night to cross."

William Faulkner has said that Hemingway, never reaching beyond himself, never achieved a grand failure. Though the reaching is admirable, it seems, on consideration, that *To Have and Have Not* was so nearly within Hemingway's grasp that a little more time would have fetched it. He would certainly have trimmed, and he might have seen Morgan as a greater Manuel or Brennan and have saved him from propaganda. Might have, but probably would have not. Hemingway could not keep his self-pity distant. But he comes close to doing so, as he puts the dying Morgan into his nearly cosmic African perception, letting the gay borrowed boat drift with the primordial Gulf Stream as the fishes swarm and eat, and then repeating the picture at the end of the book with a perfect image of the central contrast between the gay "haves" and the wary, independent, and struggling "have nots," the man alone: "A large white yacht was coming into the harbor and seven miles out on the horizon you could see a tanker, small and neat in profile against the blue sea, hugging the reef as she made to the westward to keep from wasting fuel against the stream."

7

✑ IT TOLLS FOR THEE

I N HARRY MORGAN, Hemingway had started to indict collective
society for the death of the individual, but had ended by throwing in his lot with society, just as he was in fact throwing himself
into the collective effort for Spain. He had thought, in *Green Hills,*
that "if you serve time for society, democracy, and the other things
quite young" and decline "any further enlistment," you could "make
yourself responsible only to yourself." And he had been happy
doing so. But now, with the world watching a civil war between
the haves and the have nots, he could no longer forgo the prison
of social service and "the pleasant, comforting stench of comrades."

Hemingway himself remained a reporter, of course; but his hero
becomes a dedicated soldier. The idea of self-reliance becomes a
quaint Marxist by-product: "Clearly I miss [God], having been
brought up in religion [says old Anselmo]. But now a man must
be responsible to himself." And in the end, Anselmo prays both
for others and for himself in the corporate sacrifice. Nevertheless,
for all the new corporate responsibility, Hemingway's hero remains
a man alone; and the novel fails in the same degree in which Hemingway fails to marry self and society. Moreover, the new hero
himself is flawed. Like Frederic Henry, though proportions differ,
Robert Jordan is one part defeated youth and one part undefeated
loser. Flaws notwithstanding, Hemingway's new fervor and breadth,
and his old love of Spain, make *For Whom the Bell Tolls* his biggest and worthiest novel.

War had started on July 17, 1936. By the year's end, still
working to finish *To Have and Have Not,* Hemingway had raised
$40,000 on personal notes for ambulances and medicine for the
Loyalists. By January, 1937, he was heading the Ambulance Com-
mittee of the American Friends of Spanish Democracy. Soon he
joined with old friends Dos Passos, MacLeish, and Lillian Hellman
in an organization of "Contemporary Historians" and from February 27 until May 19, 1937, was off to Spain making *The Spanish*

Earth, their documentary movie on behalf of the Spanish peasant. He spoke in Carnegie Hall to the American Writers' Congress; he showed his film at the White House.

Hemingway's second visit (August 14, 1937, to January 28, 1938) produced *The Fifth Column,* written in the Florida Hotel in Madrid under shellfire, as reporter Martha Gellhorn "sailed in and out in beautiful Saks Fifth Avenue pants with a green chiffon scarf wound around her head," according to Josephine Herbst, and as the odor of cookery from Hemingway's well-stocked room drifted through the halls. Hemingway's last two visits (March 19 to May 31, 1938; September 1, 1938, until sometime that winter) produced dispatches for the North American Newspaper Alliance, and sketches for *Ken, Esquire,* and *Cosmopolitan.* On October 14, 1938, Scribner's published *The Fifth Column and the First Forty-nine Stories,* collecting "The Capital of the World," "The Snows of Kilimanjaro," and "The Short Happy Life of Francis Macomber" for the first time, and demonstrating again Hemingway's uncertainty as to whether journalism might not be fiction by including "Old Man at the Bridge," virtually a straight report from Spain. When Madrid fell and the war ended at the end of March, 1939, Hemingway was already two weeks into *For Whom the Bell Tolls.* He finished revising, on galley proof, eighteen months later at Sun Valley, Idaho. Scribner's published it October 21, 1940.

≈§   §≈

The Fifth Column, Hemingway's only play other than "To-day Is Friday," tells of counterespionage against the Fascists' secret "column" inside Madrid, which aided the four military columns aimed at the city. Hemingway weighs one's responsibility "only to yourself" as against responsibility to society, the attractions of love and life at international resorts as against dedication to the Loyalist, Communist cause. Philip Rawlings outlines an imaginary vacation with his Dorothy much as Robert Jordan is to do with his Maria (and Colonel Cantwell with his Renata). But Rawlings half scorns the triviality he can no longer have, and Jordan makes a fancy to keep up Maria's spirits. Throughout the play, Hemingway's commitment to the cause of humanity remains slightly hypothetical, the whole coming out like Maxwell Anderson, though perhaps a little better.

Although some have said that *The Fifth Column* shows Hemingway's famous dialogue to be a poetry of the silent page, the lines often have the Hemingway verve, and certainly enough life to stand up on the stage. But the play does not take time sufficient to fill out Rawlings' hypothetical outlines. He is something of a gun-toting superman, with ideological waverings, slightly uncomfortable about his insensitivity to killing and torturing—an interesting sketch of Robert Jordan. The play ends almost like a break in a film; the original triangle has long since vanished; and Dorothy Bridges is Hemingway's thinnest daydream, however inspired by the blond Miss Gellhorn. "Her name might also have been Nostalgia," Hemingway says in his Preface. She is certainly, as Carlos Baker says, the hero's "bridge" to the past, which he leaves smoldering; but to German Max her name is "Britches," a reading equally suitable. The play has some good gunning, and an excellent inquisitor: "I could die all right. I don't ask any one to do something that is impossible"—"But to die——(*He shakes his hand in the quick triple flip of the wrist that is the Spanish gesture of supreme admiration*). To die? Priests? Terrific." We see the same Petra whom Robert Jordan is to mention as cooking for the newspapermen "at the hotel" in Madrid, perhaps drawn from life at the Hotel Florida, along with the manager and some of the others.

◆§ ⁂ ≶◆

For Whom the Bell Tolls, dedicated to Martha Gellhorn, continues the study of self versus service. But each side of the conflict has so proliferated that the conflict breaks in two, and the personal side breaks in two again. The sweets of personal life give way in the end to the specter of personal death, becoming almost a new issue entirely. The proliferation on the side of service, however, gives the novel new riches. The problem of service is complicated by a corrupt society, a hopeless predicament, a useless battle, and—somewhat as an afterthought, not clearly caught—the realization that, even in war, each of us is diminished by the death of every man, since "No man is an *Iland*," as Hemingway's epigraph from John Donne says. Here the novel is great. Had Hemingway escaped the personal and grasped the full irony of Donne's paradox in its new context of war, the novel would have been as great as its parts.

The personal cry that gave life to Nick and Jake and Frederic is no less real in Robert Jordan. It simply interferes with the breadth and depth of the book, partly in itself, partly in the introspective quavers that in the early heroes were only implications from behind sealed words. Jordan is perhaps braver than his predecessors, but the cry has become more articulate as it has moved nearer to death. The young man's illusion of immortality, however dynamited, had left Hemingway's early hero drifting but alive, with an insupportable life to support. Death had been something in the afternoon for someone else. Even as recently as *The Fifth Column*, death is for others. Philip Rawlings does not face death, nor does he consider that he will die: "We're in for fifty years of undeclared wars and I've signed up for the duration." Nevertheless, at some time after Hemingway's automobile accident (November, 1930) and the Nada of the early thirties, and immediately after the health of green hills— around the turn of Hemingway's own thirty-fifth year—death had begun to move in as an actuality. With "Kilimanjaro" and "Macomber" the question becomes that of one's own death, for which the bell tolls in anticipation, and finally tolls in fact. Every man's involvement in every man's loss ends, in Hemingway's emphasis, on a chillingly personal note: "It tolls for *thee*." If Robert Jordan had pondered the proposition that no man is an island rather than the questions of how much life one can have and of how bravely one can die, the novel might have cohered into grandeur.

But Hemingway did not decide on Donne and the tolling bell until he was almost through. He had thought to call the book *The Undiscovered Country*, perhaps thinking of the simple Spanish earth caught between Marx and Nietzsche, perhaps seeing Jordan's service to humanity as the kind of country to which an American could still go, after the geographical frontiers had blown away. Certainly the novel's strength is in its Spanish people. Pilar and Pablo are minor masterpieces—even if they are, as W. M. Frohock says, in his *The Novel of Violence in America*, extensions of Hemingway's personality. Hemingway has named Pilar after his fishing boat, which had been named apparently, and oddly, for the Blessed Virgin of Pilar, the patroness of the Fascist army (with rank of supreme general), to whom Hemingway now has the Fascist cavalryman's sister pray, as Hemingway balances good against good. Anselmo and El Sordo are equally fine. Hemingway has well used his talent, first seen in the Italian gardener in "Out of Season," for presenting in dry, sympathetic comedy a character of lower vision than the author's.

Part of Hemingway's gift of characterization is his ear for idiom. From the first he has been able to manufacture an English that seems French or Italian or Spanish, with exactly the amusing savor they would have for the fluent foreigner:

"And how is she, the *mujer* of Pablo?"

"Something barbarous," the gypsy grinned. "Something *very* barbarous. If you think Pablo is ugly you should see his woman. But
brave. A hundred times braver than Pablo. But something barbarous."

"Pablo was brave in the beginning," Anselmo said. "Pablo was
something serious in the beginning."

"He killed more people than the cholera," the gypsy said. "At the
start of the movement, Pablo killed more people than the typhoid
fever."

"But since a long time he is *muy flojo*," Anselmo said. "He is very
flaccid. He is very much afraid to die."

The characters emerge with the language, especially when it is
comic or angry. The tender moments between Jordan and his little
rabbit seem less successful. Indeed, all the *thees* and *thous,* which
have been praised as Elizabethan and epic, as they translate the
difficult Spanish *tu,* often strain credulity: "Thou askest me to take
things seriously? After what thou didst last night? When thou
needest to kill a man and instead did what you did? [asks the
gypsy]. You were supposed to kill one, not make one." The *you*
may save the passage, but it would have saved the question had it
appeared throughout. Hemingway's ear is not perfect. He slips
again into his old *would haves*: "I wish I would have had the luck
to see you before your hair was cut"—"I wish we would have spent
the last night differently." *I'd* and *we'd* would have improved these
sweet murmurs, Spanish or English. And on the last page, in his
own epic voice, Hemingway writes: "Robert Jordan's luck held very
good."

But the book is alive with the Spanish character, each person
illustrating it differently. Pilar gives us its best, its lustiness, decency, and fatalistic steadiness; Pablo its worst, its brutality and
selfish cunning; Anselmo, its simple decency; El Sordo, its bravery
and courtliness; the gypsy, its whimsicality. The Spanish character
itself, attractive and treacherous, furnishes the conflict and poses
the book's insistent question: of what worth is a sacrifice for a
people so blissfully selfish, so brutal—"he had the complete Spanish
lack of respect for life"—so unappreciative, and undependable?

A Spaniard was only really loyal to his village in the end. First Spain
of course, then his own tribe, then his province, then his village, his
family and finally his trade. . . .

Of course they turned on you. They turned on you often but they
always turned on every one. They turned on themselves, too. If you
had three together, two would unite against one, and then the two

would start to betray each other. Not always, but often enough for you to take enough cases and start to draw it as a conclusion.

"What a people," thinks Pilar. "What a people," thinks El Sordo, laughing almost to death. "What a people they have been [thinks Robert Jordan]. What sons of bitches from Cortez, Pizarro, Menéndez de Avila all down through Enrique Lister to Pablo. And what wonderful people. There is no finer and no worse people in all the world. No kinder people and no crueler. And who understands them? Not me, because if I did I would forgive it all."

Jordan is caught with the problem of the Spanish people. Where Frederic Henry had turned his back on a society disintegrating in war, Jordan faces the problem of duty and sacrifice in spite of social disintegration. He had come to Spain as soon as the war started in the summer of 1936 and had "fought that summer and that fall for all the poor in the world, against all tyranny, for all the things that you believed and for the new world you had been educated into." Jordan's new world, apparently, is the Marxist vision of the 1930's, the world in which the "have nots" eventually *have*.

Jordan is an instructor in Spanish at the University of Montana, on leave for the academic year 1936–37. He has played football: "Roll Jordan, Roll!". He has learned about dynamite on summer construction with the forestry service. He has written a book from his tramps through Spain during parts of the past ten years. He wants to write another about his serving the Republic as saboteur and assassin, since "once you write it down it is all gone"—that is, the guilt is all gone. He shares Hemingway's embarrassment over fine style: "You ought to write," he tells himself in deprecation after a flight of metaphors. Like Hemingway, he confuses journalism with fiction: Pilar tells about Pablo and the mob, and Jordan wishes he "could write well enough to write that story"— "God, how she could tell a story." Like Hemingway, he hopes he can "write a true book."

Jordan is, of course, Hemingway again, with a father who has committed suicide and a grandfather he admires. He is also something of an American dream, superb with women, guns, and dynamite. His Maria is another, this time in pastoral setting—a raped virgin, innocence within cruel experience, childlike of vocabulary, somewhat boyish of haircut, like Brett, "somewhat crazy" from the horrors of war, like Catherine. Hemingway even gives Robert and Maria a touch of that coy twinship—the same he had given Catherine and Frederic—which has marked the lovers in romances from most ancient times and which can still be seen in high-school corridors: "we could go together to the coiffeur's and they could cut it neatly on the sides and in the back as they cut mine and that way it would look better in town while it is growing out." "You could be brother and sister by the look," says Pilar. "But I believe it is fortunate that you are not."

Although Jordan's love spices the tale and complicates the sacrifice, it actually obscures the central issue. To be sure, it allows Jordan some philosophic depth, as he speculates on life and time somewhat as Hemingway had done in Africa, finding that his threescore hours and ten have been as full as a lifetime. As F. I. Carpenter has said, in Jordan's thoughts about love Hemingway is achieving the "fifth dimension" that transcends ordinary perceptions of time, mentioned in *Green Hills of Africa* and probably acquired from William James and Ouspensky via Gertrude Stein and others. And although this overview of time works well in Hemingway's contrasted simultaneous scenes, it does not work well with Jordan. It is not the central issue. The central issue is that of sacrifice—first, in the face of failure and dubious appreciation, and, second, at the cost of man's killing part of mankind. Jordan's American-Marxist idealism has been progressively disillusioned: "You are a long way from how you felt in the Sierra and at Carabanchel and at Usera, he thought. You corrupt very easily, he thought. But was it corruption or was it merely that you lost the naïveté that you started with?" At first he had seen lost comrades as noble sacrifices. But now he has seen something of Russian cynicism. His Russian friends are able, admirable, and devious. They are indifferent to killing. They are using Spain for their own ends; humanity is an impersonal "they" to be manipulated: "They cannot all be as difficult to do anything with as Spain is."

The Spanish people come to represent the intransigence of all the humanity for which one tries to sacrifice oneself, just as they also represent those people worth every sacrifice, the Anselmos, the Sordos and Pilars. But Jordan's sacrifice is doomed from the start. The Russian general who sends him out to blow up a bridge behind enemy lines in broad daylight knows that his plans will probably fail: "You know how those people are." His plan is in fact betrayed by loose Spanish talk. Pablo's treachery merely echoes the major betrayal and joins the unlucky snowfall as an inevitable impediment to the useless blowing up of the bridge "on which the future of the human race can turn." Jordan, who knows that the attack is betrayed, proceeds with the job that he knows is too late and will probably kill him. Why?

Simply that the old idealism, in spite of all disillusion, may perhaps prevail:

> You're not a real Marxist and you know it. You believe in Liberty, Equality and Fraternity. You believe in Life, Liberty and the Pursuit of Happiness. Don't ever kid yourself with too much dialectics. They are for some but not for you. You have to know them in order not to be a sucker. You have put many things in abeyance to win a war. If this war is lost all of those things are lost.

Jordan is the dogged opposite of Lieutenant Henry, throwing himself away in spite of the world's wrong, believing that somehow the useless sacrifice will help to make it right. He is also the opposite of the African Hemingway who is tempted to write America off in pursuit of his own happiness. Jordan frankly represents that American idealism which was in fact evident in Spain during the civil war, and which has not been lacking from the world's theater before and since. And like the idealism of the Abraham Lincoln Brigade, Jordan's is both somewhat Marxist and somewhat despairing: "he said it now in a complete embracing of all that would not be, 'I love thee as I love all that we have fought for. I love thee as I love liberty and dignity and the rights of all men to work and not be hungry.' "

This is bad writing, of course, embarrassing in its failure before the ideality of love and sacrifice that Hemingway is attempting. Nevertheless, Jordan's despairing idealism is tested by a doom that accumulates with artistry throughout the book. As it opens, Jordan is worried. The general's fear of Spanish instability does not make easier the daylight demolition with uncertain companions. Pablo immediately exhibits that "sadness they get before they quit or before they betray." Pilar, four-square and granitic, restores Jordan's confidence only to unseat it by refusing to say what she has read in his palm. The unstated doom in his lifeline continues to haunt Jordan and the book. An owl flies. Enemy planes come over, as Carlos Baker notes, in cabalistic "threes, and threes and threes." As Hemingway uses the natural gypsy lore of Spain, so he uses also the natural mountain springtime to underwrite Jordan's doom with both sunshine and snow. Jordan lies pleasantly on pine needles at beginning and end, the image of a dead man, as D'Agostino has said. He will kill when the enemy reaches "the sunlit place where the first trees of the pine forest joined the green slope of the meadow."

The problem of killing, the irony of killing, is the book's pivot. Jordan turns the question of killing—cold Russian, hot Spanish—around and around:

Yes, Robert Jordan thought. We do it coldly but they do not, nor ever have. It is their extra sacrament. Their old one that they had before the new religion came from the far end of the Mediterranean, the one they have never abandoned but only suppressed and hidden to bring it out again in wars and inquisitions. They are the people of the Auto de Fé; the act of faith. Killing is something one must do, but ours are different from theirs.

Though Jordan apparently does not know Donne, and never understands that "any man's death diminishes *me*," he knows that killing is wrong, and that he has enjoyed it: "admit that you have liked to kill as all who are soldiers by choice have enjoyed it at some time whether they lie about it or not." He continues to question himself:

Do you think you have a right to kill any one? No. But I have to. How many of those you have killed have been real fascists? Very few. But they are all the enemy to whose force we are opposing force. But you like the people of Navarra better than those of any other part of Spain. Yes. And you kill them. Yes. If you don't believe it go down there to the camp [where his latest victim lies]. Don't you know it is wrong to kill? Yes. But you do it? Yes. And you still believe absolutely that your cause is right? Yes.
    It is right, he told himself, not reassuringly, but proudly. I believe in the people and their right to govern themselves as they wish. But you mustn't believe in killing, he told himself. You must do it as a necessity but you must not believe in it. If you believe in it the whole thing is wrong.

This is as far as Jordan himself gets with the book's titular theme. Hemingway himself did not get further until he sensed the deepening irony behind his contrasting episodes and took Donne's idea for his epigraph and title: war is most sadly and viciously futile because each man kills part of himself—a proposition with which Hemingway would not have agreed, had he entirely understood it. Using the variety of views he discovered in *To Have and Have Not,* Hemingway gets at the real problem of the Spanish war and of any war: not the problem of enjoying killing, nor of killing people one likes, nor of how bravely one can face death without committing suicide, but the problem of "any man's death." The question runs through the book, to be sure—clearly asked but never clearly answered. It begins with Jordan's first discussion with Anselmo and continues until Lieutenant Berrendo, with whom we have lived for a moment and know to be good, walks into Jordan's sights an instant before both will be erased.

Anselmo is a Christian, thinks Robert Jordan: "Something very rare in Catholic countries." Steadfast old Anselmo hates to kill. Since "the movement" has banished religion, he hopes that the new state will organize some civic penance to cleanse its killing. He finally prays for the souls of El Sordo's band and prays that he will be firm during the attack. "But with or without God [he has said earlier], I think it is a sin to kill. To take the life of another is to me very grave. I will do it whenever necessary but I am not of the race of Pablo."

Something of Hemingway the African naturalist shows in Jordan, who does not like to kill animals, but who has found to his disturbance that he does not mind killing men. In a startling Christian image, which old Anselmo the Christian does not notice, we get intimations of the unspoken message of Donne and Robert Jordan, who is named for the river that baptized Christ: any man's death diminishes *me*. Anselmo, who hates to kill men, is proud of the bear he shot: "And every time I saw that paw, like the hand of a man, but with those long claws, dried and nailed through the palm to the door of the church, I received a pleasure." Anselmo remembers with pride the shooting of the bear, peacefully turning over a log with his human paw, on the hillside in the early spring, exactly the setting that will see both him and Jordan dead in three days' time. But Robert Jordan knows that a bear is very like a man; and clearly man has crucified him.

The book, then, proceeds, through the brutalities and animal cunning of Pablo, through the simple dedication of Anselmo, through the irresponsibility of the gypsy, and through the constancy of Pilar, to state the ultimate irony of war: it must be pursued and won by those who believe in their cause, but how ironically futile it is, since both sides believe; how grimly wrong, since each man's death, including those of the men I kill, diminishes me.

Hemingway illustrates this point toward the end in three parallel instances. The first is when Jordan, shirt off, sunning his back in a cloudless spring afternoon, reads the letters of the young cavalryman he has killed and listens to the shots from where El Sordo is surrounded. The cavalryman had been, like Jordan, in love, like

Jordan, with a cause: "doing away with the Reds to liberate Spain from the domination of the Marxist hordes."

The second is the magnificent death of El Sordo—whose real name is Santiago and whose courtly courage will pass to the Santiago of *The Old Man and the Sea*. Old and deaf at fifty-two, angry at having to die (and on such a day) but accepting it, laughing as if to split his aching head and arm at the arrogant young officer who shouts, not knowing he will die, "Shoot me! Kill me!," El Sordo sees the mutual death of shooter and shot as an excruciating yet somehow tender joke: "Yes, Comrade Voyager. Take it, Comrade Voyager"—making natural poetry of his Marxist Spanish. (Earlier Hemingway's Spaniards have used "voyage"—*viaje*—for a danger-ous trip, over the bull's horn or into the guns.) "What a people," Sordo thinks, and we know he is sharing Pilar's earlier thought: " 'What a people the Spaniards are,' I said to him. And what a people they are for pride, eh, *Ingles*? What a people." We re-member also that Jordan, too, is a voyager toward death, since the Fascist captain has an odd face for a Spaniard, "the face of an *ingles*."

The third demonstration of the irony in the mutual voyage comes as Lieutenant Berrendo, calling his own decapitations barbarous, though necessary for identification and effect, prays for the soul of his dead friend:

> He went on with the prayer, the horses' hooves soft on the fallen pine needles, the light coming through the tree trunks in patches as it comes through the columns of a cathedral, and as he prayed he looked ahead to see his flankers riding through the trees.

And just then Anselmo sees them, and leaves to make *his* prayer, in his fear, for Sordo and the others and himself, and to hear Fer-nando say, "What barbarians these fascists are!"

Hemingway, with his alternating views, indeed matches Tolstoy—in spite of Hemingway's later assertion to Lillian Ross that "no-body's going to get me in any ring with Mr. Tolstoy unless I'm crazy or I keep getting better." "I love *War and Peace*," Heming-way wrote in his "Introduction" to *Men At War*, "for the wonder-ful, penetrating, and true descriptions of war and of people. . . ." As Andrés carries Jordan's message, we see war's muddle, from guerrilla through trooper to general staff, in brilliant flashes that equal Tolstoy's Borodino, illustrating the peculiarly Spanish in-difference and callousness that gives the book its plot, gathering the suspense and frustration, putting a crescendo behind the irony of man's killing man and diminishing himself.

Again Hemingway cannot keep the great human irony free of private pathos. Again he almost brings the two together. Jordan is not the man Harry Morgan is. He is too much the mere self, idealized—a transparency of clear ego. Hemingway could survey Morgan from above and, except at the end, keep him far enough away as "character" to see him. He could keep Morgan's mind sufficiently shut to stay undefeated. But Hemingway gives Jordan no distance at all. Jordan is so close as to be walking right within our daydreams, and we sometimes cannot see him at all. His mind is opened to the doubts that spell defeat at the very time he takes the undefeated stance.

As Jordan's early life drifts through his mind, we are convinced of what we have known all along: he is our old friend Nick Adams and our old friend Frederic Henry, our former defeated youth, now cast in the role of undefeat. He is a cross between Hemingway's two conflicting modes, his two types of hero, never to be reconciled: the young man crushed and defeated by a world he did not make and cannot understand, and the older battered survivor whom many crushings cannot defeat, partly, one is tempted to say, because he does not know any better.

Jordan, like the typical defeated Hemingway youth, does know better. He knows too much; he thinks too much, though, like his predecessors, he tries to shut thought off. The ghost of his father's suicide haunts him and spoils both the grand irony and the personal dauntlessness as he lies in agony on pine needles waiting for Berrendo to reach the sunlit mountain grass. Hemingway's private fear of fear, his personal outcry against a world that does not give us what we want and then kills us in the bargain, damages his presentation of the supreme irony of war that sets good young men killing other good young men to their mutual loss.

But Hemingway has come some distance from Frederic Henry. Although war is still senseless, although the individual is still trapped and alone—off by himself behind enemy lines with a handful of dissidents—commitment is now necessary in spite of the dark, and there is now a strong sense of other individuals and of the irony in their mutual losses. In 1942, Clifton Fadiman, Sinclair Lewis, and Sterling North chose *For Whom the Bell Tolls* for the Limited Editions Club as the American novel that "most clearly approaches the stature of a classic." It certainly makes the approach.

8

❧ THE OLD MAN

YOUNGER MEN and women come to him for advice about their literary problems and their love affairs, while he talks to them as if he were ninety years wise instead of only forty-nine," wrote Malcolm Cowley of his old friend Hemingway in an article published in January, 1949, a few months before Hemingway was to begin *Across the River and Into the Trees,* the first of his two portraits of the hero as an old man. Hemingway's image of himself as nobly beaten beyond his years, and still undefeated, had long been abuilding. Count Mippipopolous of *The Sun Also Rises,* enjoying his champagne, exhibiting his black chest and his welted Abyssinian arrow scars, is an outline of the figure Hemingway himself progressively liked to cut, though with fewer wars and revolutions on his tally than the Count's seven and four. He was already "Beery-poppa" at the age of twenty-four, to Hadley; and "Papa" at thirty-four to Marlene Dietrich. In *Green Hills,* at thirty-five, he was playing Poor Old Papa to his Poor Old Mama; and his admiration for Pop, the British hunter, splendid beneath the grizzle and fallen muscle, no doubt helped to age the private image. Colonel Cantwell is almost a dittoed copy of Hemingway's interior and exterior decoration, a Nick Adams antiqued for the role of undefeat. But Santiago of *The Old Man and the Sea* comes from Hemingway's objective mode, an aged but undefeated Manolo lifted to heroic dimensions.

By this time, of course, Hemingway had, like Count Mippipopolous, "been around a very great deal." Like the Count, he had continually fallen in love. "The best writing is certainly when you are in love," Hemingway was to tell Plimpton. The dedicatory page of each of his love stories bears the name of a different wife: Hadley for *The Sun Also Rises,* Pauline for *A Farewell to Arms,* Martha for *For Whom the Bell Tolls,* Mary for *Across the River and Into the Trees.* The Spanish war and the Florida Hotel had removed Hemingway from Pauline and approximated him to Martha Gellhorn, also a girl of wealthy family, also a journalist formerly of the Paris staff of *Vogue,* and also, like Hadley and Pauline, from St. Louis. In spite of their Catholicism and their mutual efforts to save the marriage, Pauline and Hemingway had divorced on November 4, 1940. He had married Martha on November 21 at Cheyenne, Wyoming, and the two had gone off to cover the Sino-Japanese war. Since Pauline had kept the Key West villa, the new Hemingways had settled in Cuba at *Finca Vigia* ("Lookout Farm"), twelve miles from Havana, a fifteen-acre estate previously rented during *For Whom the Bell Tolls.*

World War II had again recessed Hemingway's writing, had again ended one marriage and provided another. Hemingway had volunteered his *Pilar* to U. S. Naval Intelligence, and had cruised off Cuba with an armed crew of nine, pretending to fish and planning to capture a submarine if one should hail him. He had accepted a job with *Collier's* (for whom Martha was covering the Mediterranean) and had hitched a ride to London with the RAF. He had ridden on RAF missions over Germany, had impaled his head on a rear-view mirror in a blacked-out automobile wreck in London, and had finally reached the European front, stationing himself alternately with French guerrillas and with Colonel C. T. Lanham, whose regiment he saw slaughtered in Huertgen Forest, and whom Hemingway was to imagine himself to be as he created Cantwell in *Across the River.*

Hemingway had played soldier so assiduously—armed with gin, vermouth, grenades, and other exterminators—that French irregulars had thought him a disguised general and the U. S. Army had called him on the carpet. He had romped into Paris, not ahead of the French, as his own version would have it, but actually tagging along in his jeep with a slightly scrambled column of General Leclerc's armor, as General S. L. A. Marshall, who was with him, has pointed out in "How Papa Liberated Paris," in the *American Heritage.* Nevertheless, Hemingway was soldiering a bit, pointing out targets to the tanks, taking men to a roof near Sylvia Beach's Shakespeare and Company to kill snipers, and leaving the impression that he had "liberated" the cellar of the Ritz, though the manager was already greeting old friends in the foyer when Hemingway arrived. Hemingway's driver met others at the door with: "Papa took good hotel. Plenty good stuff in cellar." Hemingway had set out, with Leclerc's group, from Rambouillet, a name famous for a seventeenth-century campaign of refinement that conditioned the French and

English languages for the next three centuries. In his own refinement of the unrefined, the new innovator from Rambouillet may equal the record, as his influence on both French and English writing already suggests. "Plenty good stuff in cellar."

The Ritz had also brought Hemingway Mary Welsh, the second feminine war correspondent into Paris, whom he married in Havana on March 14, 1946, having divorced Martha there on December 21, 1945. Sometime later, the Ritz was to turn up a trunk, stored years before, containing forgotten notebooks from the twenties, from which Hemingway wrote *Paris Sketchbook*, only to call it back from Scribner's for revision six months before his death. Also short of final publication at his death was *The Dangerous Summer*, his revisit to Spain and bullfighting published serially in *Life* (beginning September 5, 1960). But more important, the end of the war had seen Hemingway return to a magnum opus, begun before Pearl Harbor, several volumes of which he eventually deposited in his Havana bank. *Across the River and Into the Trees* is an excursion from this work; *The Old Man and the Sea* is its coda.

❧ ❧

In February, 1949, a fragment of shotgun wadding had entered Hemingway's eye unnoticed during a duck-shoot near Venice. A few days later, blood poisoning hospitalized him in Padua and nearly took his life. As he recuperated, he wrote the story of the duck-shooting colonel, the fifty-year-old veteran with a bad heart and a nineteen-year-old mistress. *Cosmopolitan* serialized it from February to June, 1950; Scribner's published it September 7.

Carlos Baker has shown how *Across the River and Into the Trees* is a curious love affair of the battered but unbowed Cantwell with his former youth, in the person of the Venetian Countess Renata ("reborn"), aged exactly the nineteen of Cantwell-Hemingway's wounding into life in the First World War, and of his first view of Venice, the lovely city. Baker has also shown how failing machinery, from motorboat to elevator, echoes Cantwell's own failing heart and unsteady current as he inhales the cold winds from the mountains of death to keep alive. The book is Hemingway's most consciously literary. Cantwell himself is full of quotations. He is a walking irony of undefeated loss. His first name, Richard, suggests "the lion-hearted," as Renata says; and his last name says that the leonine heart *Can't* get *Well*.

But under the tough contrivance, the irony is heavily narcissistic and pathetic. Cantwell is Nick Adams older but hardly wiser—Hemingway again imagining himself the soldier he was not quite. Cantwell even has a touch of Krebs, though Hemingway is now more accustomed to the strain of putting himself into fiction, truly.

> "You ought to write," the girl said. "I mean it truly. So some-one would know about such things."
> "No," the Colonel disagreed. "I have not the talent for it and I know too much. Almost any liar writes more convincingly than a man who was there."

As in *To Have and Have Not*, a writer is pictured as the falsest of the false, in a searing caricature of Sinclair Lewis that is also a war-scarred alter-image of Cantwell-Hemingway, for whom Cantwell, despite the soft place in his heart for all the crippled and wounded, has nothing but contempt. Lewis' remarks, thirteen years before, that Hemingway was both puerile and senile had hurt, because, as Cantwell and Hemingway were both demonstrating, the remarks were uncomfortably close to the truth.

Cantwell is something of a compendium of Hemingway's auto-biographical heroes. Like Nick propped against the church or Jake who cannot pray, he is a truncated Christian. Renata dreams that his wounded right hand "was the hand of Our Lord"; he thinks he might "run as a Christian" toward the end, but knows that he will not. Like Adams, Henry, and Barnes, Cantwell tries not to think, "as he had thought of nothing so many times in so many places. But it was no good now. It would not work any more because it was too late." As in *The Sun Also Rises*, the lovers sweetly cannot marry; as in *A Farewell to Arms*, the lady wants to "be you"; as in *The Fifth Column* and *For Whom the Bell Tolls*, the man outlines a vacation he knows they will not take.

Like Nick on his bicycle, Cantwell goes up the sunken road to "the last and saddest rebuilt house in Fossalta," beyond which, as a young lieutenant in the Italian army "he had been hit, out on the river bank." Here, where he and Nick and Hemingway had left their mutual knee cap thirty years before, Cantwell squats to relieve himself and deposits also a 10,000 lira note, an amount equal to the pension on his Italian medal for twenty years, leaving an ambiguous monument to his former self (ten years and 5,000 lira short of full repudiation, however), as if, like Nick, he felt that he had not fully earned his glory.

"A poor effort . . . But my own," says Cantwell, as he buttons up, in his opening salvo of literary commonplaces. One allusion, not so commonplace, illuminates a puzzling reference way back in

"The Three Day Blow," in the first "Nick" stories, and tightens the connection between Nick Adams and Dick Cantwell. In the story, Bill has discussed literature with Nick, and has called him "Wemedge." Nick, newly drunk, looks in the mirror and finds his face strange. The mystery in "Wemedge" vanishes when we find Cantwell, a steady drinker, looking at *his* face in the mirror and paraphrasing a description of Wemmick in Dickens' *Great Expectations*. Dickens describes Wemmick's "square wooden face, whose expression seemed to have been imperfectly chipped out with a dull-edged chisel." Cantwell says, of *his* face: "It looks as though it had been cut out of wood by an indifferent craftsman." Nick had been, playfully, a "Wemedge"; Cantwell is now more seriously a Wemmick. Hemingway, it would seem, had read Dickens in boyhood (presumably at the age of Nick in "The Three Day Blow") and is again recalling Dickens' memorable caricature, remembering the simile and the manner but not the precise wording. Hemingway's caricature of Sinclair Lewis as the American journalist, with face like "an over-enlarged, disappointed weasel or ferret" and "black hair that seemed to have no connection with the human race" (Lewis had red hair; Hemingway had black), also reveals in Hemingway an unusual and new touch of the Dickensian hyperbole.

Hemingway's favorite lines from Quinet and Villon, as Carlos Baker has shown, now appear on Cantwell's lips: *fraîche et rose comme au jour du bataille* and *Où sont les neiges d'antan?*—both picked up from friends and conversation (the first from Joyce). So, one suspects, was the famous epigraph to Eliot's "Portrait of a Lady," which had given Hemingway the title of "In Another Country," and its ironic reference to fornication and a wench now dead. Bill Gorton had played on it wildly in *The Sun Also Rises*. Jake had introduced him facetiously as a taxidermist, and Bill had added: "That was in another country. . . . And besides all the animals were dead." Now Cantwell makes a cruelly close reference to Hemingway's Martha Gellhorn:

> "But that was in another country and besides the wench is dead."
> "Is she really dead?"
> "Deader than Phoebus [sic] the Phoenician. But she doesn't know it yet."

Eliot's Phlebas from "The Waste Land" and his dead wench from "Portrait of a Lady" are exactly the references that, in the twenties, a generation excited by Eliot's new volume, would have been batted about.

Similarly, Hemingway's tags from Blake, Whitman, and Shakespeare seem more conversational than erudite. But *Othello* had been in Hemingway's mind with Frederic and Catherine in *A Farewell to Arms*, and again in *Green Hills*. Now Hemingway builds an elaborate Shakespearean parallel: "They were not Othello and Desdemona, thank God, although it was the same town and the girl was certainly better looking than the Shakespearean character, and the Colonel had fought as many, or more times than the garrulous Moor." The garrulous Cantwell also charms his lady, also considerably younger, with tales of his exploits. He buys her a pin, of the kind everyone wore "in the old days in this city and the faces were those of their confidential servants." But the pin of the old city also represents Othello: a "little negro, or moor, carved in ebony with his fine features, and his jeweled turban."

The Shakespearean parallel is distant, however, and merely decorative, as is another: the making of Renata to represent both Venice, the former "queen of the seas," and Venus, the Queen of Love, who was born from the sea, as Stewart Sanderson has noted in his *Hemingway*. Cantwell asks her if she would "like to run for Queen of Heaven," apparently a reference to Venus' famous beauty contest. although Catholic Renata thinks the idea sacrilegious. The portrait of "reborn" Renata looks like Botticelli's famous painting of Venus' birth from the sea: the portrait's hair is "twice as long as it has ever been and I look as though I were rising from the sea without the head wet." The bartender who presides over Cantwell's rendezvous with his Goddess of Love is one Cipriani, a true modern priest of the Cyprian Venus.

But all the contrivance cannot hide much silliness, as Cantwell talks to his girl's portrait or as she gives him the family jewels for comfort in his pocket; it cannot cover some downright hilarity, as when Cantwell calls his girl "Daughter" and "his voice was thickened a little," as he says it. Hemingway's autobiographical projection is never more damaging. Cantwell at his worst is most like the Hemingway Lillian Ross describes arriving in New York in late 1949 with the manuscript of *Across the River and Into the Trees* under his arm, calling everyone "daughter," shadowboxing about the room as he describes the job of writing, wing shooting with imaginary shotgun at pigeons in the middle of Fifth Avenue, downing hypertension pills with his champagne, putting his fist to his cheek to block an imaginary punch, as he shakes his shoulders in silent laughter to indicate a joke, repeating the formulas that now substitute for conversation: "Crowd a boxer. . . . Duck a swing" —"I have seen all the sunrises there have been in my life, and that's half a hundred years" (Cantwell's very phrase). Hemingway the man becomes increasingly pathetic, as the lost boy continues to stare out from the grizzled caricature of age. As Edmund Wilson said of him much earlier in his "Hemingway: Bourdon Gauge of Morale," Hemingway himself is "certainly the worst-invented character to be found in the author's work. If he is obnoxious, the effect is somewhat mitigated by the fact that he is intrinsically incredible."

Although the book stands somewhat more firmly than the man, Cantwell is again the pathetically insecure Hemingway. He has scarred and toughened his hide to no avail (Cantwell's scars and Hemingway's, like Nick's and Henry's of an earlier era, tally as on a physician's chart). He must strain for a sexual triple in a gondola, to the near breakage of his heart, and, affectionately calling himself "You beat-up old bastard," must still check his feared inadequacy in a mirror, as Barnes had done his actual one: "We are hung as we are hung, for better or worse, or something, or something awful." With Cantwell, as with Hemingway, everything is an act, even within the act, as the mirror fails to catch the self. Cantwell must constantly think about what others think of him, now strutting, now scoffing at himself, as he puts on his "soldier suit" and (like Hemingway) takes a corner table to protect his flanks.

For a while the act holds, since all men must sometimes ponder how they appear to others. Cantwell worries plausibly about his boatman's surliness, and plausibly puts it aside as he determines to make the last shoot of his life as good as the poor conditions allow. The duck shooting is a perfectly natural allegory of Cantwell's determination to live in active scorn of imminent death. As Young has pointed out, the passage over dark water at the edge of death, with a gloomy boatman, makes a perfectly natural and eerie Stygian impact, authenticated by a later reference to Dante. For a while Hemingway can objectify Cantwell, as he had objectified himself in *Green Hills*: "He went out, walking as he had always walked, with a slightly exaggerated confidence, even when it was not needed, and, in his always renewed plan of being kind, decent and good, he greeted the concierge. . . ."

For a while Cantwell's inner monologue holds, in its witty self-depreciation: "And what is a tough boy, he asked himself. . . . I suppose it is a man who will make his play and then backs it up. Or just a man who backs his play. And I'm not thinking of the theatre, he thought. Lovely as the theatre can be." The tough boy and the aesthetician are both humorously in balance, before

Cantwell wobbles into bravado and honey. So it is with Cantwell's Secret Order, played with the *maître* of that most fortunately-named of all hotels, the Gritti Palace. The Order is amusing, and perfectly represents the cynical amity of the battered, whose real relationship is no deeper than that of restaurateur and familiar guest. It is good for a pleasant entry to the dining room, but Cantwell can't well give up the play.

Across the River began as a short story, Hemingway told Lillian Ross ("That's the way all my novels got started"), and as a short story it might well have held. The Colonel shooting at first, and dying at last, is solid, and even moving, as Hemingway conveys the suppressed dread of death by heart attack, faced as bravely as any-one can face it. Robert P. Weeks has pointed out the pathetic irony in having Cantwell die as young Jackson sits practical and indifferent in the front seat, an ironic opposite of the old Stonewall Jackson whose dying words Cantwell quotes (to give the book its title). The tragic irony of death is that in the universal experience everyone is alone; the audience, as in Hemingway's high-school foot-ball poem, is always remote, and relatively indifferent. And in Cantwell's death, Hemingway's self-pity flashes out into a general sympathy for our lonely lot, from which we Can't get Well, as the world drives on. Cantwell dies undefeated, except by the dreams of love (everything about Renata has been a remembrance while duck shooting), and the brave self-pity, that have split both him and the book apart. Like Harry of Kilimanjaro, he is a version of the childish dream of seeing oneself dead and mourned to the pun-ishment of all the unappreciative. Our attention shifts from brav-ery to regret, indeed to resentment against the dirty trick of being born for this. Like Jordan, Cantwell fails as undefeated loser be-cause he has too much of the self-consciousness that makes cowards of us all.

"I am a strange old man," said the fifty-year-old Hemingway to Lillian Ross, apparently repeating one of his facetious catch phrases. "I am a strange old man," says Santiago, who, like Hemingway, suffered from "the benevolent skin cancer the sun brings," but who is unbearded and actually old—"except his eyes and they were the same color as the sea and were cheerful and undefeated." Two years after what seemed the debacle of *Across the River*, Hemingway pulled himself together, like an undefeated loser himself, and pro-

ERNEST HEMINGWAY AT A NEWS CONFERENCE FOLLOWING
NOBEL PRIZE ANNOUNCEMENT, 1954

duced his most nearly perfect book. In the old fisherman he was able to objectify his self-image of age. He returned again to his objective mode. He again reduced the hero's understanding and self-consciousness to that of a simple, uneducated man. The hero is again like little Manolo of "The Undefeated."

Hemingway was able to objectify his hero because he had, as with Manolo and Jack Brennan, an actual person other than himself in mind. Fifteen years before, as Young has pointed out, Hemingway had written in *Esquire* (April, 1936) of a Cuban fisherman:

> Another time an old man fishing alone in a skiff out of Cabañas hooked a great marlin that, on the heavy sashcord handline, pulled the skiff far out to sea. Two days later the old man was picked up by fishermen sixty miles to the eastward, the head and forward part of the marlin lashed alongside. What was left of this fish, less than half, weighed eight hundred pounds. The old man had stayed with him a day, a night, a day and another night while the fish swam deep and pulled the boat. When he had come up the old man had pulled the boat up on him and harpooned him. Lashed alongside the sharks had hit him and the old man had fought them out alone in the Gulf Stream in a skiff, clubbing them, stabbing at them, lunging at them with an oar until he was exhausted and the sharks had eaten all that they could hold. He was crying in the boat when the fishermen picked him up, half crazy from his loss, and the sharks were still circling the boat.

Hemingway was to modulate this toward magic, and to make it the coda of his unpublished magnum opus. Leland Hayward had persuaded Hemingway to publish it separately in *Life* and to turn it into a movie. Hemingway had known it was good. It won him the Pulitzer Prize (postponed from *For Whom the Bell Tolls*) in 1953, and the Nobel Prize in 1954. "I tried to make a real old man, a real boy, a real sea and a real fish and real sharks. But if I made them good and true enough they would mean many things," said Hemingway (*Time,* December 13, 1954).

He does, of course, give the tale conscious touches of the mythical, changing the actual two days into the mysterious three of fairyland and Christianity, having Santiago cry out as a man might, "feeling the nail go through his hands and into the wood." Hemingway has again crucified man, as Young has said, and in what Waldmeir has called a "religion of man," borrowing from Christianity to make endurance noble. As Melvin Backman, following Robert M. Brown, has pointed out in his "Hemingway: The Matador and the Crucified," "Santiago" means "Saint James," the "fisherman, apostle, and martyr from the Sea of Galilee." Moreover, there are suggestions of Calvary, as Carlos Baker says, in the old man's struggling up the hill and falling under the weight of his mast, and further suggestions of the Crucifixion in his strange—if not physically impossible—position as he lies down to sleep: on his stomach, "with his arms out straight and the palms of his hands up." The boy weeps at the sight of the wounded hands.

But perhaps more important is Hemingway's changing of the actual events into a story of undefeat. The real old man had been crying and "half crazy from his loss." Santiago is the perfection of Hemingway's undefeated loser: " 'But man is not made for defeat,' he said. 'A man can be destroyed but not defeated.' " His patched sail looks "like the flag of permanent defeat"—that is, it is still sailing, still flying, in the very teeth of defeat. The old man has faith. He loves, and is loved by, a boy he has taught to fish. The boy is Manuel—the name both of the bullfighter of "The Undefeated" and of the Messiah (Santiago names him only in the diminutive, "Manolin"). The boy's father has forbidden him to go fishing with the old man after forty luckless days.

> "He hasn't much faith," [the boy says.]
> "No," the old man said. "But we have. Haven't we?"
> "Yes," the boy said.

The faith, of course, is in one's own ability, one's endurance, one's undefeated courage. The boy is the old man's messiah of strength and hope. "I'll bring the luck with me," he tells the old man. As Carlos Baker has said, the boy is also the old man's disciple, associated in his mind with lions seen once in his youth in Africa. "He only dreamed of places now and of the lions on the beach. They played like young cats in the dusk and he loved them as he loved the boy." At the end, sitting in the road, trying to get up from where he has fallen under the mast, the old man watches a cat pass "on the far side going about its business." And in the last sentence of the book, he is asleep "dreaming about the lions."

The lions, as Young has said, playing like cats on the white beach, have something in them of Harry's literary leopard on white Kilimanjaro; and certainly, as shown in Hemingway's Nobel Prize remarks about the greatness of the past driving a writer "far out past where he can go, out to where no one can help him," *The Old Man and the Sea* is an allegory not only of man's general effort but also of Hemingway's personal effort, as a writer, to prevail. The lions certainly also have connections with that fine picture of courage, the dying lion in "The Short Happy Life of Francis Macomber." Africa and lions perfectly represent Hemingway's own younger happiness in Africa, now seen from the very Gulf Stream he had thought about in African fields.

But the curiosity of lions on the beach at Casablanca, certainly never seen in historic times, suggests another source, coming perhaps, like Dickens, from Hemingway's youth: Robinson Crusoe also was impressed by great cats, and one lion, at dusk on the western beaches of Africa, where Defoe, too, had imported them from a more fabulous interior. A remark reported by Aronowitz and Hamill in their *Ernest Hemingway* suggests that in 1950 (two years before *The Old Man and the Sea*) Hemingway—with his luxurious estate on the island of Cuba, not far from Crusoe's own Caribbean island— was thinking facetiously of himself as Robinson Crusoe: "What difference does it make if you live in a picturesque little outhouse surrounded by three hundred feebleminded goats and your faithful dog Black Dog? The question is: can you write?" The goats, of course, suggest Crusoe, with the faithful Friday merged with Crusoe's dog ("Blackdog" was the actual name of Hemingway's spaniel). But whatever the source, the power of lions, the questions of writing, of man alone, are certainly energizing *The Old Man and the Sea* as the defeated fisherman endures, and dreams of lions.

Loss and undefeat are in almost perfect balance. Unlike Morgan, Jordan, and Cantwell, Santiago does not die. With the huge skeleton tied to his skiff, he has brought the proof of his victory home. His courage and endurance are registered with awe among his fellow fishermen—"There has never been such a fish"—and he goes to sleep dreaming of those images from his youth of brave indomitable power, which he in his spirit retains and has just demonstrated with the same kind of self-effacing commitment to the duty of being a man that Jack Brennan, the prizefighter of "Fifty Grand," had shown. Old Santiago, too, might have said, "It was nothing." As Weeks and Baker have said, the loneliness of Santiago's victory in loss gets a final ironic grandeur through the indifferent cat and the incomprehensive tourists who see the great carcass and think it only a shark. As with Cantwell, we see that man, enduring only in himself, as he must in Hemingway's world and in any world, must suffer alone as the world goes about its business.

The story has been and will be widely admired. The line of suspense and loss is almost perfectly arched, spoiled only when

Santiago chats with himself like another Jordan or Cantwell or Hemingway, wishing he could feed the fish, who is his brother, wondering what it would be like if a man had to kill the sun and moon each day, thinking about luck:

> "I'd like to buy some if there's any place they sell it," he said.
> What could I buy it with? he asked himself. Could I buy it with a lost harpoon and a broken knife and two bad hands?
> "You might," he said. "You tried to buy it with eighty-four days at sea. They nearly sold it to you too."
> I must not think nonsense he thought.

This is painfully cute, like much of the aging Hemingway himself. But the comic irony of the old man's simple view can also be marvelous, as in his mystique of baseball and the wonder of Di-Maggio's bravery, a mere nothing beside the old man's own, which he takes as a matter of course. For the most part, Hemingway gets out of himself and catches in the natural line of events some paradigm of the greater suspense and mystery of life.

The great fish, unseen under water, the slanting line moving the boat with unseen power, is exactly the way it is with fishing and exactly the way it is with myth. "The fish never changed his course nor his direction all that night as far as the man could tell from watching the stars." Again, as in his early stories, Hemingway can render a simple, natural statement symbolic: "The dark water of the true gulf is the greatest healer that there is"; "Sail on this course and take it when it comes"; "He must pull until he dies." Again and again, the fish seems "strange," as indeed a big fish does:

> At one time when he was feeling so badly toward the end, he had thought perhaps it was a dream. Then when he had seen the fish come out of the water and hang motionless in the sky before he fell, he was sure there was some great strangeness and he could not believe it. Then he could not see well, although now he saw as well as ever.

By holding to the simple perceptions of a simple man, and by regaining the Biblical pulse of his early prose, along with the indistinct Biblical references, Hemingway has kept his tale realistic and yet given it exactly enough of the mysterious to make it seem a parable or a fable or a fairy tale illustrating something true about the essential life of man. So it is with the suspense in which first, hope against hope, the fish is hooked (we expect at least a loss or two before the big contest). So it is with the sharks, when the fish is finally in and we have experienced the triumph without seeing the losses to come. The huge skeleton and tiny skiff still sail in the reader's mind long after both are beached. Even Santiago's memory of his unbelievable twenty-four-hour handwrestling contest with the Casablanca Negro is both a sharp reality and an archetype of undefeat, the two men locked eye to eye, blood under the fingernails, the Negro's shadow, huge on the bright blue wall, moving as the wind moved the lamps—simple perceptions of the simple, illustrating something true about the life of man.

What they illustrate is the simple beauty of courage and endurance, when it is uncomplicated by other and more intricate moral issues. They illustrate that life is a perpetual proof, as with courage, or virtue, or even with the business of being a writer. One cannot really rest on laurels. "I will show him what a man can do and what a man endures. . . . The thousand times that he had proved it meant nothing. Now he was proving it again. Each time was a new time. . . ." Hemingway's message, as always, is simple; but it is true, and even noble. He says, simply, that a man must endure this life, must be brave in the teeth of its challenges, even unto death, to sail on this course and take it when it comes. If a man does this, he will remain undefeated no matter what he loses.

For once, in a major work, Hemingway was able to free himself from the old self-pity, the old resentment against the world for not being as one would wish it, or against life for leading us to death. For once, he accepts life. Within his intellectual limits, never broad nor deep, he has written a positive existential fable for the mid-twentieth century.

"The dark water of the true gulf is the greatest healer there is." It was the only healer Hemingway knew, except for such palliatives as liquor, war, ritualistic violence, and the homeopathic medicine of writing. All his life he feared some inner gulf of Nothing, around which he swirled. With only nerve to sustain him, he feared a lack of nerve. Was he really brave? Could he really take the ultimate test? These seem to have been the perpetual questions. His first story, written in high school, had dealt with suicide, by gunshot, to avoid an agonized death. When his father committed suicide with his grandfather's Civil War pistol to avoid suffering, the questions obviously grew louder. Both Harris in "Homage to Switzerland" and Jordan in *For Whom the Bell Tolls* suggest Hemingway's anxious resentment, the fear that he, like his father, would fail the test. Robert Jordan had become physically ill when he learned that his father was a coward, probably in an incident similar to that which produced "The Doctor and the Doctor's Wife." From *The Fifth Column* onward, the question of bravery under torture seems to have lurked in Hemingway's mind—who had seen disemboweled horses and writhing game with relative indifference, and the leg-breaking of horses at Smyrna with horrified fascination. Philip Rawlings weighs his insensitivity to the torture of prisoners, and Colonel Cantwell has apparently done some torturing himself ("in obtaining his exact knowledge he had not fulfilled the complete spirit of the Geneva Convention"). Jordan accepts the irony in Pilar's and Maria's assumption that his father had killed himself to escape inquisition rather than merely a painful illness. "Nobody Ever Dies!" (*Cosmopolitan*, April, 1939) is about a Cuban Joan of Arc going to her torture bravely.

Perhaps at the end, suffering from physical hypertension and mental depression, with a hint of the diabetes that had moved his father to suicide, Hemingway had a sense of paying his father a debt of understanding, and of moving by fate in the same eddy, the one he had so long feared. Perhaps he simply consoled himself with taking action, with the momentary immortality in the god-like giving of death that he had found in the killing of bulls and antelope, as he put the muzzles of his silver-inlaid shotgun in his mouth and tripped both triggers early on the morning of July 2, 1961, just short of his sixty-second birthday. It was the ultimate act of self-pity, a mercy killing of the poor self by the self, in the teeth of all it had been. Hemingway had arrived the night before at his home near Ketchum, Idaho, after release from his second visit to the Mayo Clinic, where he had received shock treatments for depression. "There is no lonelier man in death, except the suicide. . . ."

Whatever may come from the vaults of Havana, *The Old Man and the Sea* is the place to end. It makes positive the gulf of Hemingway's despair. It is a triumph of will and intuition from the man slipping into the gulf. It is a remarkable product from the pathetic man, with his deprecatory Indian talk—which goes all the way back to "Fathers and Sons" and Trudy of upper Michigan ("Long time ago good. Now no good.")—whom Lillian Ross saw in 1950, and the even more pathetic man whom Seymour Betsky and Leslie Fiedler saw in 1960, sick, fragile, and almost inarticulate. *The Old Man and the Sea* makes a good conclusion. In the early style, it brings to rest the undefeated loser, dreaming of lions.

⊰ ⊱

Like *Green Hills*, the posthumous *A Moveable Feast* (the *Paris Sketchbook* newly entitled) is an autobiographical assessment and debt of love, which Hemingway at last pays to Hadley, so studiously omitted from the early fiction they lived for. As in *Green Hills*, a person says he cannot remember someone, and Hemingway promises to put him in a book: this time, Fitzgerald, almost as erratic and ephemeral as his splintering wife. Stein, Ford, and Pound appear in swifter sketches. But the most insistent presences are those of the fiction, the shades of the people and places we have come to know (and Hemingway characteristically invites us to take *this* as the fiction, if we so wish). We discover, for instance, that Hadley, omitted from the first novel, got into the second after all, as Hemingway, like Henry, lies uneasily awake with his wife sleeping "sweetly now with the moonlight on her face." The life and the fiction contain the same tiny, buried bubble of emptiness.

Here also is "The Big Two-Hearted River," written so intensely, at a table in a clean, well-lighted place, that Hemingway slips an arm from his remembered pack to sharpen his pencil. Here is the private mystery of writing, invoked by labor, done in a spell, and shut from thought in the afternoon strolls, with a secret chestnut and worn rabbit's foot in the pocket. At first the incantation is just faintly pidginish and faintly repetitious—*The Sun* and *Death* warmed over. But the anecdotes grow firmer, the prose fades to beauty, the people stand clear, until—just before the bubble finally burst—we end high in the Alps with Hadley, with the glory of the downhill rush over glaciers, and Bumby, and sunlight, and youth, "when we were very poor and very happy."

◦§ §◦

Looking back down the line, one can see Hemingway's shift from the poetry of defeat to that of undefeat, with a brief sociological engagement midway in a long succession of men alone, and with something of a clash between the subjective, autobiographical meditation and the objective observation. Hemingway's hero is essentially a man alone, against lowering circumstances. Hemingway's power, as well as his uncertainty, comes from this self-glorifying and romantic isolation, seeing oneself singled out for Promethean punishment. His obsession with truth comes from the secret knowledge that, glorifying himself as a ruined Adams, or Adam, he is being personally untruthful. His is the agony of Krebs, whose true accounts seem false because too bland, and whose glorifications turn to dust in his mouth. He had appropriated Moise's hobo adventures as his own to impress Canadian friends. He had told Sylvia Beach that he had spent two years in a hospital recuperating from a wound for which priests had almost performed last rites, and that he had had a bitter boyhood because his father had died tragically (some years before his father's actual death), leaving him only a gun and the task of supporting his mother, brothers, and sisters.

Throughout his life, in fiction and out, Hemingway mentions mental unsoundness, and there can be no doubt that his brain had been frequently drowned within and battered from without. In 1958, he told Plimpton that he had received "two concussions and a skull fracture" during one year in Madrid; in 1949, he mentioned before Lillian Ross "seven concussions in two years," in addition to one breaking open of the head and one pushing of a rear-view-mirror support through the front of the skull. Remarks by Jake Barnes and Lieutenant Nick, as well as by Hemingway himself, suggest that perhaps Hemingway sometimes really could not, or would not, distinguish between his real and his imagined activities. He seems always to have been holding himself up for inspection, and then turning away from what he was afraid he would see, obsessed with himself, and haunted by his feared inadequacies.

When he could personify these in Nick Adams, at the Two-Hearted River, or lying awake benumbed by fear in another country, he wrote as true a cry of lost youth in a lost world as anyone will ever write. The language is stretched tight with all the implications of sadness and terror it does not state. The same is true of Jake Barnes in *The Sun Also Rises*, Hemingway's only unflawed novel before *The Old Man and the Sea*, the first and the last.

As the century grew older, so did Hemingway. Despair turned to existential courage; the beaten youth gave way to the older un-defeated loser. Hemingway's existentialist attitude emerged with his objective mode, his portraits of lower life, and produced three superb works—"The Undefeated," "Fifty Grand," and *The Old Man and the Sea;* against these we may balance the perfection of the early inner cry—"In Another Country," "Now I Lay Me," and *The Sun Also Rises*. To make up the best of Hemingway, we should also add his last two significant stories, the best products of his African adventure and social concern, "The Short Happy Life of Francis Macomber" and "The Snows of Kilimanjaro." But then we cannot forget the near-greatness of the Tolstoian *For Whom the Bell Tolls*. Nor can we forget the shrewd and humorous ironies of boyhood, as when, in "Ten Indians," Nick is "awake a long time before he remembered that his heart was broken." And then we remember the tender, tight despair of "A Clean, Well-Lighted Place," and the grand voyage toward death of El Sordo on the hilltop in the sun.

For all of Hemingway's grave personal uncertainty, which forced him to act out and write out a life he did not understand, for all of the poverty in what he has to say—that man is ironically caught alone in a world that will kill him, and that he can either move numbly in defeat or bravely in invincibility—for all these limits and indeed because of them, Hemingway has written a remarkable shelf-full of stories and books, which can often catch, beautifully and forever, a simple but essential irony of existence in a simple prose resonant with the pity and terror of it all.

SELECTED BIBLIOGRAPHY

Note: (P) indicates works available in paperbound edition.

HEMINGWAY'S CHIEF WORKS

Three Stories and Ten Poems. Paris and Dijon: Contact Publishing Company, 1923.
in our time. Paris: Three Mountains Press, 1924.
In Our Time. New York: Boni and Liveright, 1925. (P)
The Torrents of Spring. New York: Charles Scribner's Sons, 1926.
The Sun Also Rises. New York: Charles Scribner's Sons, 1926. (P)
Men without Women. New York: Charles Scribner's Sons, 1927.
A Farewell to Arms. New York: Charles Scribner's Sons, 1929. (P)
Death in the Afternoon. New York: Charles Scribner's Sons, 1932.
Winner Take Nothing. New York: Charles Scribner's Sons, 1933.
Green Hills of Africa. New York: Charles Scribner's Sons, 1935. (P)
To Have and Have Not. New York: Charles Scribner's Sons, 1937.
The Fifth Column and the First Forty-nine Stories. New York: Charles Scribner's Sons, 1938.
For Whom the Bell Tolls. New York: Charles Scribner's Sons, 1940. (P)
Men at War, The Best War Stories of All Time, edited, with an Introduction by Hemingway. New York: Crown Publishers, 1942. (P)
Across the River and into the Trees. New York: Charles Scribner's Sons, 1950.
The Old Man and the Sea. New York: Charles Scribner's Sons, 1952.
A Moveable Feast. New York: Charles Scribner's Sons, 1964.

UNCOLLECTED STORIES AND POEMS

"Judgment of Manitou," *Tabula* (Oak Park High School, Illinois), XXII (February 1916).
"A Matter of Colour," *Tabula* (Oak Park High School, Illinois), XXIII (April 1916).
"Sepi Jingan," "How Ballad Writing Affects Our Seniors" (poem), *Tabula* (Oak Park High School, Illinois), XXIII (November 1916).
"The Worker" (poem), "Athletic Verse" (poem, with Fred Wilcoxen, in

three parts: "The Tackle," "The Punt," "The Safety Man"), "The Inexpressible" (poem), *Tabula* (Oak Park High School, Illinois), XXIII (March 1917).

"Wedding Gifts" (poem), Toronto *Star Weekly* (December 17, 1921).

"A Divine Gesture," *Double-Dealer* (New Orleans), III (May 1922).

"Ultimately" (poem), *Double-Dealer* (New Orleans), III (June 1922).

"They All Want Peace. What Is Peace?" (poem), *Little Review* (Paris), IX (Spring 1923).

"The Soul of Spain with McAlmon and Bird the Publishers, Part I" (poem), "The Earnest Liberal's Lament" (poem), *Der Querschnitt* (Frankfurt), IV (Autumn 1924).

"The Age Demanded" (poem), *Der Querschnitt* (Frankfurt), V (February 1925).

"Nothoemist Poem," *Exile Magazine* (Paris), I (Spring 1927).

"Valentine, For a Mr. Lee Wilson Dodd and Any of His Friends Who Want It" (poem), *Little Review* (Paris), XII (May 1929).

"The Denunciation," *Esquire,* X (November 1938).

"The Butterfly and the Tank," *Esquire,* X (December 1938).

"Night Before Battle," *Esquire,* XI (February 1939).

"Nobody Ever Dies," *Cosmopolitan,* CVI (March 1939).

"Under the Ridge," *Cosmopolitan,* CVII (October 1939).

"The Good Lion," "The Faithful Bull," *Holiday,* IX (March 1951).

"Two Tales of Darkness: A Man of the World; Get a Seeing-Eyed Dog," *The Atlantic Monthly* (November 1957).

DOCUMENTARY FILM

The Spanish Earth. Produced by Contemporary Historians (an organization including Hemingway, Lillian Hellman, John Dos Passos, Archibald MacLeish): July 8, 1937. Script published as a book, *The Spanish Earth.* Cleveland: J. B. Savage Company, 1938.

SELECTED NONFICTION

"And to the United States. The Quarter. Early Spring," *Transatlantic Review* (Paris), I (May–June 1924).

"And Out of America," *Transatlantic Review* (Paris), II (August 1924).

"Pamplona Letter," "Conrad," *Transatlantic Review* (Paris), II (October 1924).

"Homage to Ezra," *This Quarter* (Paris), I (May 1925).

"My Own Life," *The New Yorker,* February 12, 1927.

"The Real Spaniard," *The Boulevardier* (Paris), I (October 1927).

"Who Knows How," in Henry Goodman's *Creating the Short Story.* New York: Harcourt, Brace & Company, 1929.

"Who Murdered the Vets?" *The New Masses,* XVI (September 17, 1935).

"Wings Always over Africa, An Ornithological Letter," *Esquire,* V (January 1936).
"On the Blue Water, A Gulf Stream Letter," *Esquire,* V (April 1936).
"On the Madrid Front, Hemingway Reports Spain," *New Republic,* XC (May 5, 1937; reports continue January 12, April 27, June 8, 1938).
"The Clark's Fork Valley, Wyoming," *Vogue,* XCII (February 1939).
"On the American Dead in Spain," *The New Masses,* XXX (February 1939).
"How We Came to Paris," *Collier's,* CXIV (October 7, 1944).
"Safari," *Look,* January 26, 1954.
"The Christmas Gift," *Look,* April 20, May 4, 1954.
"The Dangerous Summer," *Life,* September 5, 12, and 19, 1960.

BIBLIOGRAPHY

Baker, Carlos. "A Working Check-List of Hemingway's Prose, Poetry, and Journalism—with Notes," *Hemingway, The Writer as Artist.* Princeton, N.J.: Princeton University Press, 1956.
Samuels, Lee. *A Hemingway Check List.* New York: Charles Scribner's Sons, 1951.

SELECTED BIOGRAPHIES

Anonymous. "The Hero of the Code," *Time,* July 14, 1961.
Anonymous. "Life with Papa," *Time,* November 8, 1954.
Aronowitz, Alfred, and Peter Hamill. *Ernest Hemingway, The Life and Death of a Man.* New York: Lancer Books, Inc., 1961.
Beach, Sylvia. *Shakespeare and Company.* New York: Harcourt, Brace & World, Inc., 1959.
Betsky, Seymour. "A Last Visit," *Saturday Review,* Special Hemingway Issue, July 29, 1961.
Callaghan, Morley. *That Summer in Paris.* New York: Coward-McCann, Inc., 1963.
Cowley, Malcolm. "A Portrait of Mister Papa," *Life,* January 10, 1949.
Eastman, Max. "The Great and Small in Ernest Hemingway," *Saturday Review,* April 4, 1959.
Fiedler, Leslie. "An Almost Imaginary Interview: Hemingway in Ketchum," *Partisan Review,* XXIX (1962).
Hemingway, Leicester. *My Brother, Ernest Hemingway.* Cleveland: The World Publishing Company, 1962.
Hemingway, Mary. "Hemingway, A Personal Story by the Great Writer's Wife," *Look,* September 12, 1961.
Hotchner, A. E. *Papa Hemingway.* New York: Random House, Inc., 1966.
Knoll, Robert E. (ed.). *McAlmon and the Lost Generation, A Self-Por-*

trait, ed. with a commentary by Robert E. Knoll. Lincoln, Neb.: University of Nebraska Press, 1962.

Loeb, Harold. *The Way It Was*. New York: Criterion Books, Inc., 1959.

Marshall, S. L. A. "How Papa Liberated Paris," *American Heritage*, XIII (1962).

Plimpton, George. "An Interview with Ernest Hemingway," *The Paris Review*, XVIII (1958); in Carlos Baker, *Hemingway and His Critics*.

Porter, Katherine Anne. "A Little Incident in the Rue de l'Odéon," *The Ladies' Home Journal*, August 1964.

Ross, Lillian. "How Do You Like It Now, Gentlemen?" *The New Yorker*, May 13, 1950; in Robert P. Weeks, *Hemingway*.

Sanford, Marcelline (Hemingway). *At the Hemingways, A Family Portrait*. Boston: Little, Brown & Company, 1962.

Schreiber, Georges. *Portraits and Self Portraits*. Boston: Houghton Mifflin Company, 1936 (portrait by Schreiber; one-page autobiography by Hemingway).

Stein, Gertrude. *The Autobiography of Alice B. Toklas*. New York: Harcourt, Brace & Company, 1933.

Young, Philip. "Hemingway and Me: A Rather Long Story," *Kenyon Review*, XXVII (1966).

CRITICAL AND INTERPRETATIVE STUDIES

Biographical Criticism

Baker, Carlos. *Hemingway, The Writer as Artist*. Princeton, N.J.: Princeton University Press, 1956.

Fenton, Charles A. *The Apprenticeship of Ernest Hemingway, The Early Years*. New York: The Viking Press, Inc., 1954.

Rovit, Earl. *Ernest Hemingway*. New York: Twayne Publishers, Inc., 1963.

Young, Philip. *Ernest Hemingway*. New York: Holt, Rinehart & Winston, Inc., 1952.

Anthologies

Baker, Carlos. *Hemingway and His Critics, An International Anthology* (with bibliography of criticism). New York: Hill & Wang, Inc., 1961.

McCaffery, John K. M. *Ernest Hemingway: The Man and His Work*. Cleveland: The World Publishing Company, 1950.

Weeks, Robert P. *Hemingway, A Collection of Critical Essays* (with selected, annotated bibliography of criticism). Englewood Cliffs, N.J.: Prentice-Hall, Inc., 1962.

Selected Criticism

Anderson, Charles R. "Hemingway's Other Style," *Modern Language Notes*, LXXVI (1961).

Angstrom, Alfred. "Dante, Flaubert, and 'The Snows of Kilimanjaro,' " *Modern Language Notes*, LXV (1950).

Backman, Melvin. "Hemingway: The Matador and the Crucified," *Modern Fiction Studies*, I (1955).

Bartlett, Phyllis. "Other Countries, Other Wenches," *Modern Fiction Studies*, III (Winter 1957–58).

Beebe, Maurice. "Criticism of Ernest Hemingway: A Checklist with an Index to Studies of Separate Works," *Modern Fiction Studies*, I (1955).

Brooks, Cleanth. *The Hidden God: Studies in Hemingway, Faulkner, Yeats, Eliot, and Warren*. New Haven, Conn.: Yale University Press, 1963.

Burhans, Clinton S., Jr. *"The Old Man and the Sea: Hemingway's Tragic Vision," American Literature*, XXXI (1960).

Carpenter, Frederic I. "Hemingway Achieves the Fifth Dimension," *PMLA*, LXIX (1954); reprinted in his *American Literature and the Dream*. New York: Philosophical Library, Inc., 1955.

Clendenning, John. "Hemingway's Gods, Dead and Alive," *Texas Studies in Language and Literature*, III (1962).

Colburn, William E. "Confusion in 'A Clean, Well-Lighted Place,' " *College English*, XX (1959).

Cowley, Malcolm. Introduction to *The Portable Hemingway*. New York: The Viking Press, Inc., 1944.

D'Agostino, Nemi. "The Later Hemingway," *Sewanee Review*, LXVIII (1960).

Eastman, Max. "Bull in the Afternoon," *The New Republic*, LXXV (June 7, 1933).

Evans, Oliver. " 'The Snows of Kilimanjaro': A Revaluation," *PMLA*, LXXVII (1962).

Flanagan, John T. "Hemingway's Debt to Sherwood Anderson," *Journal of English and Germanic Philology*, LIV (1955).

Frohock, W. M. *The Novel of Violence in America, 1920–1950*. Dallas, Texas: Southern Methodist University Press, 1950.

Gerstenberger, Donna. *"The Waste Land* in *A Farewell to Arms," Modern Language Notes*, LXXVI (1961).

Graham, John. "Ernest Hemingway: The Meaning of Style," *Modern Fiction Studies*, VI (1960).

Gurko, Leo. "The Old Man and the Sea," *College English*, XVII (1955).

Halliday, E. M. "Hemingway's Ambiguity: Symbolism and Irony," *American Literature*, XXVIII (1956).

Keeler, Clinton. *"A Farewell to Arms: Hemingway and Peele," Modern Language Notes*, LXXVI (1961).

Killinger, John. *Hemingway and the Dead Gods.* Lexington, Ky.: University of Kentucky Press, 1960.

Kroeger, F. P. "The Dialogue in 'A Clean, Well-Lighted Place,' " *College English,* XX (1959).

Levin, Harry. "Observations on the Style of Ernest Hemingway," *Kenyon Review,* XIII (1951).

Lewis, Robert W., Jr. *Hemingway on Love.* Austin, Tex.: University of Texas Press, 1965.

Light, James F. "The Religion of Death in *A Farewell to Arms,*" *Modern Fiction Studies,* VII (1961).

Marcus, Fred H. *"A Farewell to Arms:* The Impact of Irony and the Irrational," *English Journal,* LI (1962).

Mazzaro, Jerome. "George Peele and *A Farewell to Arms:* A Thematic Tie?" *Modern Language Notes,* LXXV (1960).

Moses, H. K. "Water, Water, Everywhere: *Old Man* and *A Farewell to Arms,*" *Modern Fiction Studies,* V (1959).

Moynihan, William T. "The Martyrdom of Robert Jordan," *College English,* XXI (1959).

Oldsey, Bern. "The Snows of Ernest Hemingway," *Wisconsin Studies in Contemporary Literature,* IV (1963).

Poore, Charles. "Foreword and Twelve Brief Prefaces," *The Hemingway Reader.* New York: Charles Scribner's Sons, 1953.

Reinert, Otto. "Hemingway's Waiters Once More," *College English,* XX (1959).

Sanderson, Stewart. *Hemingway.* Edinburgh and London: Oliver and Boyd, 1961.

Spilka, Mark. "The Death of Love in *The Sun Also Rises,*" in Charles Shapiro, ed., *Twelve Original Essays on Great American Novels.* Detroit: Wayne State University Press, 1958.

Stephens, Robert O. "Hemingway's Old Man and the Iceberg," *Modern Fiction Studies,* VII (Winter 1961–62).

Stone, Edward. "Hemingway's Waiters Yet Once More," *American Speech,* XXXVII (1962).

Sylvester, Bickford. "Hemingway's Extended Vision: *The Old Man and the Sea,*" *PMLA,* LXXXI (1966).

Waldmeir, Joseph. "Confiteor Hominem: Ernest Hemingway's Religion of Man," *Papers of the Michigan Academy of Science, Arts, and Letters,* XLII. Ann Arbor, Mich.: University of Michigan Press, 1956; in Robert P. Weeks, *Hemingway.*

Warren, Robert Penn. "Ernest Hemingway," *Kenyon Review,* IX (1947); repr. as Introduction, *A Farewell to Arms* (New York 1953).

Weeks, Robert P. "Fakery in *The Old Man and the Sea,*" *College English,* XXIV (1962).

———. "Hemingway and the Spectatorial Attitude," *Western Humanities Review,* XI (1957).

Young, Philip. "Our Hemingway Man," *Kenyon Review,* XXVI (1964).

INDEX

Note: Fictitious characters are entered in small capital letters.

Index

Index